Kenneth F. Dougherty, S.A., Ph.D., S.T.D.

Cosmology

An Introduction to
the Thomistic Philosophy
of Nature

❊❊❊

GRAYMOOR PRESS, PEEKSKILL, NEW YORK

1965

Imprimi Potest:

BONAVENTURE KOELZER, S.A.

Superior General

Nihil Obstat:

JOHN A. GOODWINE, J.C.D.

Censor Librorum

Imprimatur:

TERENCE J. COOKE, V.G.

New York, N.Y., September 29, 1965

The Nihil Obstat and Imprimatur are official declarations that
this book is free of doctrinal or moral error. No implication is
contained therein that those who have granted the Nihil Obstat and
Imprimatur agree with the contents, opinions or statements expressed.

1st Edition, October, 1952

2nd Edition, September 1953

3rd Edition, September, 1956

2nd Printing, February 1958

4th Edition September, 1965

Japanese Edition: University of Sophia,
Tokyo, Japan, 1959.

Library of Congress No. 65-28329

Designed and Printed at Graymoor Press

To My Students

Foreword

TO THE FIRST EDITION

THE DEMAND for texts in Scholastic Philosophy continues. It is an indication of vitality in the field both on the part of the teachers and of the ever increasing student body. This demand is most evident in those areas of philosophy that have closest contact with the physical sciences.

The field of Cosmology has evidenced this demand for new texts in a special way because of the manifold problems it has faced. The orbit of Cosmology in the New Scholasticism, its relation to old scholastic traditions and principles and its contacts with contemporary natural sciences have created new discussions and a need for a new presentation.

Dr. Kenneth Dougherty, S.A., in this new text, incorporates the results of thorough research and successful teaching. The work is Thomistic in spirit, keen in its recognition of the needs and the limitations of the present-day student, and sensible in its emphasis on basic principles and problems. Simplicity of language and arrangement and depth of analysis make this a most acceptable text for college students.

Fr. Ignatius Smith, O.P.
Dean of the School of Philosophy
Catholic University of America

CONTENTS

INTRODUCTION

PART ONE

THE INTRINSIC PRINCIPLES OF MOBILE BEING

SECTION ONE

Contents *continued*

Contents *continued*

A Critique of Cosmology in the Study of Nature

I. DEFINITION OF COSMOLOGY

A. NOMINAL DEFINITION. The term *cosmology* is derived from the classical Greek words *cosmos*, and *logos*. *Cosmos* means order or good arrangement. According to tradition it was first applied to the universe by the Greek philosopher Pythagoras (?-c. 500 B.C.). Plato explains in the dialogue *Gorgias* that the universe is called *cosmos* because it is ordered and governed justly:

> And philosophers tell us, Callicles, that communion and friendship and orderliness and temperance and justice bind together heaven and earth and gods and men, and that this universe is therefore called Cosmos or order, not disorder or misrule, my friend.[1]

The suffix *logy* of the word *cosmology* is from the Greek word *logos* which signifies word, or mental expression in the act of knowing. In a special sense it means reasoned knowledge and so it has come to mean science: the knowledge of things through their causes. Thus the word *cosmology* from *cosmos* and *logos* signifies the science of the universe. Aristotle called this science *Physics*, which is to be distinguished from modern physics, and the medieval Scholastics called it *The Philosophy of Nature*, a term which is once again coming into use.

The name *cosmology* was first used by Christian von

---

[1] *Gorgias*, 508, A.

Christian Von Wolff

Wolff in 1731. He wrote a philosophical work called *Cosmologia Generalis*. Wolff adopted the theories of the philosopher-scientist Gottfried Leibnitz, combined them with certain Aristotelian tenets, and partially modified them himself. He is the author of the well-known division of philosophy into ontology, cosmology, psychology and rational theology. Although modern Scholastics very often use these terms, the real meaning given to them is not the same as that intended by Wolff.

Frederick Hoyle, the Cambridge University astronomer, has popularized the name *cosmology* in his recent work on *The Nature of the Universe.*[1] In this context cosmology signifies an explanation of the evolution of the universe as a modern scientist understands it. Experts in the experimental sciences often adopt the term in this meaning. Their favored position in our times permits them to give currency to this understanding of cosmology. Just as psychology is understood by many to mean only experimental psychology rather than to extend also to rational or philosophical psychology, so also cosmology is accepted by many to be the sole property of the theorist and experimentalist in modern physics. Cosmology as a word, therefore, means the science of the universe. It is subject to various kinds of definitions as to its real significance. In this text we shall explore the science of cosmology in its philosophical content.

B. REAL DEFINITION. A science always begins with wonder. The awakening mind of every one in childhood is endowed with this natural wonder about the world. "Why is the sky blue?" the child queries. "Where did the world come from?" These and innumerable other expressions of wonderment excite the child's mind. If in the course of time they almost cease to be in the minds of many, it is because adult indifference often narrows the horizon of this natural curiosity.

Cosmology begins with wonder about the universe of changeable beings, beings in sensible matter and motion. This embraces the microcosmic world of the atom, the heavenly bodies, minerals, plants, animals and men. All these beings are called mobile beings because they are subject to various kinds of change.

Our universe abounds in contingence, an ever unfolding complex of unity and diversity of the same and the different, of

---

[1] F. Hoyle, *The Nature of the Universe* (N.Y.: Harper Bros., 1950).

the old and the new. Human life progresses from infancy to childhood and to youth, from maturity to old age and finally death. The seed becomes the plant, and the plant withers and decays into the inorganic. The elements combine into compounds and compounds dissolve into elements. Stars grow cold while other stars are born. The universe is a process of building up and breaking down. Generation follows upon corruption and corruption upon generation. There are changes *of* things, substantial changes, as in the generation of a substance and the corruption of a substance. There are changes *in* things as in their qualitative and quantitative characteristics. Finally, there are local changes, the transposition of bodies in space and time. Our cosmos is an evolving world, beings in evolution. But what is this evolution? This it the problem of change, of mobile being.

Generation, corruption, qualitative, quantitative and local changes—these are the general mobilities that man notes in the finite beings of the universe which are called mobile beings. In unriddling this mystery of the mobile universe man seeks to go to the very heart of the nature of the mobile. Man naturally wonders about the architecture of the universe itself, the nature of this ordered arrangement of mobile beings, its origin, essence and destiny. It is the special task of the cosmologist to treat these fundamental problems in a scientific manner.

Aristotle clearly distinguishes scientific knowledge from opinion. In his *Posterior Analytics* we find the following classical text on the meaning of science:

> We suppose ourselves to possess unqualified scientific knowledge of a thing as opposed to knowing it in an accidental way in which the sophist knows, when we think we know the cause on which the fact depends, as the cause of that fact and no other, and further, that the fact could not be otherwise than it is.[1]

We are convinced that we understand a thing which has causes and principles when we understand what its causes and principles are. Cosmology seeks to render the universe of mobile being intelligible in the light of its first causes and principles, which are the necessary sources of mobile beings, of their coming into being and our knowledge of them.

By first principles, strictly speaking, we mean principles

---

[1] *Post Anal.*, Bk. 1, ch. 2, 71b, 9-12.

that are immediately derived from being or reality; such as the principle of non-contradiction: it is impossible for a thing to be and not to be at the same time. The first principles of being are studied in metaphysics. In cosmology we study the first principles of mobile being. These are called first principles in a restrictive sense; namely, first in reference to the universe of mobile beings. Thus, *we define cosmology as the science which considers the first principles and causes of mobile being in general.* We shall now proceed to examine the meaning of the definition of cosmology by an analysis of its subject, object and method.

C. SUBJECT OF COSMOLOGY. The subject of a science is that about which it is concerned. Cosmology is concerned with the universe of mobile being, being in sensible matter and motion. It studies the organic and the inorganic world. It is as much concerned about the atom as it is about the heavenly body of the greatest magnitude. Cosmology can be said to share its subject with the experimental sciences of nature: physics, chemistry, geology, biology and the rest. The reason is that the common subject of all these sciences is being in sensible matter and motion.

It is incorrect to say that scientific data are the subject matter of cosmology. The subject that is considered is simply being in sensible matter and in motion. This subject when it is viewed according to the methods of the experimental sciences becomes what is commonly termed "scientific data." Scientific data are the facts of nature analyzed quantitatively and qualitatively. Thus, water is a natural subject for chemical analysis; as scientific data we have H_2O. Mobile beings are the common subject of the philosophical and experimental sciences of nature. The subject matter is itself pre-scientific; it is, so to speak, the raw material of nature.

At the beginning of the *Commentary on the Second Book of the Physics of Aristotle,* St. Thomas Aquinas contrasts natural things with artificial things. These latter have no principle of change in them except accidentally. Natural things have in themselves a principle of motion and they compose the subject of the natural sciences in general.

In his *Commentary on the First Book of the Physics,* St. Thomas affirmed:

The philosophy of nature is about natural things; but those things are natural whose principle is nature and *nature is the principle of rest and motion* in that in which it is; therefore *natural science is about those things which have in themselves a principle of motion.*[1]

Let us take a simple example: A bird is a subject of natural science because it is a being mobile by nature since it evidently has within itself the principle of motion proper to its kind. An airplane is not a natural thing, a mobile being of the cosmos; rather it is in the order of artificial things along with rocket ships. Its principle of motion is accidental to the natural substances that compose it. The natural substances that constitute the airplane are so arranged by man so as to achieve flight in the air. Aircraft propulsion, therefore, is the proper object of a specialized branch of technology rather than natural science. Artificial beings do not comprise the subject of natural science either philosophical or experimental.

This distinction between the natural and the artificial is of capital importance precisely because it sometimes happens that modern man becomes so enrapt in his world of machines that the natural world does not sufficiently command his attention in its reality as natural. Whereas some of our contemporaries look with disdain at the Medievals who, they charge, read the books of Aristotle rather than the great book of nature, we shall see that the danger in our age is to confuse the artificial with the natural, technology with the sciences of nature.

Although cosmology and the other sciences of nature share a common subject, namely, mobile being, they study it with different objects in view. We shall now investigate what constitutes the object of cosmology or what it uniquely seeks to know in the universe of mobile being.

D. OBJECT OF COSMOLOGY. Every science has something in common with other sciences. It also has something unique and peculiar to itself. When we speak of the object of a science, we mean that which it alone seeks to know about its subject or what it alone renders intelligible in its subject. The object of cosmology is the first principles of mobile being. Cosmology is distinct among the sciences because it seeks to know mobile being itself, the basic answer to the riddle of the cosmos. The one end of

[1] In 1 *Phys.*, lect. 1, n. 3.

this science is to master the meaning of that grade of being which is in sensible matter and in motion.

The science of mobile being itself is the science of the first principles of mobile being, namely its universal four causes. The cosmologist strives to know what Aristotle terms the material and the formal causes (the internal causes) and the efficient and the final causes (the external causes):

1. The material cause—that (from) which a thing is made. Brick, mortar, wood and stone are the material causes of a house.

2. The formal cause—that (in) which the thing is constituted; that which gives determination to the material in some definite way. The architecture of a house is its formal cause.

3. The efficient cause—that (by) which the thing is produced. The man who builds his own house is said to be its efficient cause.

4. The final cause—that on account of which a thing is made. When a man builds a house to shelter his family, this is its final cause.

The cosmologist seeks to know the universe of mobile being according to these four causes which were first clearly formulated by Aristotle and then improved upon principally by St. Thomas Aquinas. The cosmologist seeks to know the universal essence of mobile being: the material cause of this mode of being, from what is it made? And its formal cause, in what is it constituted? He also seeks to know its origin or its efficient cause: by what agent is it brought into being? and its final cause: on account of what is the mobile universe brought into being?

Here it is well to note that the cosmologist is not seeking to know simply the essence of mobile being or that which makes it to be what it is, but also the efficient and final causes of mobile being. St. Thomas Aquinas does not consider cosmology to be merely a study of the doctrine of hylomorphism, the doctrine of matter and form. In his *Commentary on the Physics of Aristotle* he wrote, "... the philosopher of nature demonstrates by all the causes."[1]

It is not uncommon for the student to consider the object of this study to be a course in General Science. The student who has had no previous training in philosophy is apt to evaluate

[1] In 1 *Phys.*, lect. 1, n. 5.

cosmology as an association of the discoveries of the various experimental sciences which results in an over-all view of the universe. Such an opinion judges the knowledge of mobile being as such to be a sum of our knowledge of individual mobile beings. This is not the case. Cosmology is not seeking a composite picture of the discoveries of the experimental sciences.

Just as the elaborate architectural form of a skyscraper cannot be attributed to the specialized work of the carpenters, masons and steel workers but formally to its architects so, in an analogous way, the basic meaning of mobile being cannot be attributed to a summing up of all the specialized knowledge of the experimentalists concerning the classes of mobile beings and their properties. The knowledge of mobile being itself is the special object of the cosmologist.

The physicist studies energies; the geologist, the earth's surface; the astronomer, the heavenly bodies. Each branch of experimental science studies mobile being in some of its phases and analyzes its properties. But no experimental science studies mobile being itself. These sciences describe what such and such a mobile being does under certain circumstances, but the common subject of all these sciences, the reality in sensible matter and motion, is not rendered intelligible.

St. Thomas Aquinas explains the priority of cosmology (or the *Physics* as Aristotle called it) over the other sciences about nature in the following passage:

> Because those things which follow something commonly must be treated first and separately lest we be required to repeat those things many times in discussing all parts of the common aspect, it was necessary in natural science that we have one book in which we treat those things which follow mobile being in general ... This treatise is in the book of the Physics. ... Its subject is mobile being simply.[1]

Although the experimental sciences of our modern age far surpass their crude state in the Middle Ages, these sciences can never abstract mobile being itself. They are confined to the level of the secondary and proximate principles of classes of mobile beings rather than the first principles of mobile being as mobile.

Experimental science does not reflect upon the mode of

---

[1] In 1 *Phys.*, lect., 1, n. 4.

being which it analyzes in the laboratory. It is not concerned with such basic problems as the following: What is a mobile being? Are motion and the being that moves one and the same essentially? Is the being that moves a static something to which motion is conjoined from without? Is the being that moves an essential composition of an active and static principle? What is the meaning of quantity and quality? What are space and time? Are quantity and body the same thing? Why should mathematics play such an important role in experimental science? How is quality related to mobile being? Is time the same as motion? Is space as real as the bodies that occupy space? What is the origin of the universe of mobile being? Is there purpose in the universe; if there is, what is it?

Physics and other experimental sciences do not answer these questions because these sciences do not raise them. The chemist is satisfied to study the composition and decomposition of bodies, the astronomer to study the heavenly bodies in their kinds and their various properties. The experimental scientists use the concepts of motion, and something that moves, which they call body; they employ such concepts as quantity, quality, space and time. The experimentalist uses these concepts. They are the initial concepts with which he works in his particular science but it is not his task to reflect upon them.

Each science has its unique object which it seeks to understand. No science can go everywhere in the field of knowledge. The nuclear physicist does not attempt to dissect butterflies by the use of the cyclotron, nor does the biologist attempt to cut through the atom by the use of the scalpel. It would be ridiculous for the physicist to attempt to examine the first principles of nature through physics, which is meant to examine certain secondary principles of mobility.

The attempt to make a science search after objects beyond its own proper object may be called the fallacy of the uniform method. It is not uncommon in our times to find physicists and other experts who endeavor to cross the frontiers of their particular science and establish themselves as authorities in fields where they do not belong. We shall discuss this fallacy in the forthcoming section.

The rise of the new physics at the turn of the century, when dynamic characteristics of mobile being were unfolded in the discoveries of the sub-atomic world, led to the fad of "the new cosmologies." These cosmologies of the energists, E. Mach, an Austrian physicist, M. Ostwald, a German chemist, and others, viewed all reality as purely dynamic. The *communist dialectic of nature* was later proclaimed by the English scientist, John B. Haldane, and the Soviet dean of physicists, A. F. Joffe, among others, as proven by the new physics, and all true scientists were called upon to view reality as an infinite process unfolding endlessly in space and time.

The confusion between the object of physics and the object of cosmology is not effected by people who are anxious to be confused. It is due at least in part to the failure to grasp the distinction between what physics seeks to prove and what cosmology seeks to prove. In other words, scientists with little or no training in philosophy set out to philosophize physics.

There is a hunger in every man for philosophy. The human intellect is not satisfied with mere observation and measurement. It is not satisfied with the secondary and proximate. It seeks to know the primary and the ultimate. But the mind untrained in the science of the primary and ultimate can easily mistake its object—the history of human thought bears testimony to this fact. Just as a man cannot become a physicist through the ways of common sense alone but only by studying physics, so also the physicist cannot become a philosopher without adopting the method of philosophy in the light of its proper object.

It is of capital importance for the beginner in cosmology to note well this difference between a philosophy of nature and modern physics. One *must distinguish* clearly the problems of these distinct sciences. What is the speed of light? Is light a wave or a particle? What is meant by an electrical charge? These and other questions that concern the specific kinds of mobile beings and their specific properties are the province of the physicist. The cosmologist, in contrast, is concerned with mobile beings as such. He studies this subject with the definite object in view, to render mobile being intelligible in its universal and basic meaning.

Before concluding this reflection on the object of cosmology, it is well that we note its abstract universal nature. It is not uncommon for the student to evaluate the science of mobile being as such as unreal. After all, mobile being as such does not exist. It is this or that mobile being that exists. One can perceive the mobile beings of sensible experience, the people that one meets, the trees on the campus, the birds in the air, the stars above. But mobile being itself is an abstract concept in the mind. Are we to conclude with Thomas Hobbes, the 17th century English philosopher, that abstract concepts are nothing more than names?

Of course it is true that mobile being itself does not exist except in the mind, but it has a real foundation because it is abstracted from the mobile beings of experience. It is a universal concept, and universals do not exist as such outside the mind. It is erroneous, however, to call the universal simply unreal. The true universal gives a basic report on the real beings to which it refers. The universal concept of mobile being may be compared to a window in the mansion of science through which man looks beyond the sensible to the inner reality of the mobile, mobile being in its four causes.

In conclusion, the object of cosmology is an abstract, universal mode of scientific knowledge. It extends to the entire cosmos and pertains to what is most fundamental in the origin, constitution and destiny of all reality in sensible matter and motion. The way by which the cosmologist arrives at his object, the knowledge of mobile being as such, is called the method of cosmology. We shall now proceed to examine this method.

E. METHOD OF COSMOLOGY. Every science has a unique method by which it achieves its unique object. When we say that a science achieves its object, we mean that it renders its object intelligible. Thus cosmology is terminated when it renders mobile being intelligible through the four causes. The method whereby this is achieved is both inductive and deductive.

Unfortunately some histories of science still date the beginning of induction from the experiments of Friar Roger Bacon at thirteenth century Oxford. They neglect the essential dependence of all scientific deduction upon induction in some way. The deductive character of cosmology is evident from the syllogistic process of its proofs and in the use of what the Medievals called *scientia propter quid* or demonstration through the proper causes. However, Aristotle and St. Thomas emphasize that causes are known from the things of nature which are evident as through their effects.[1] Consequently there is a definitely inductive character to this form of reasoning.

The method of cosmology is inductive because it begins with the facts of nature apprehended by the senses. The philosopher of nature cannot spin his cosmology out of thoughts about possible worlds; the subject of his inquiry is the actual cosmos in which he lives. He must begin with the world as he experiences it. This experiential knowledge is the take-off point for his abstractions about mobile being itself. As Aquinas states:

> And that natural things are moved, can be manifested from induction; because it is evident to the senses that natural things are moved.[2]

Human knowledge begins with the senses. There are many of our contemporaries, however, who disclaim sense knowledge as untrustworthy. They put all their trust in the precision of machines. For these specialists it is the machine that offers certainty to man in his quest for truth. They assert that inductive method begins and ends with the apparatus of the laboratory. In fact there are some extremists who assert that some machines can think. This trend is represented in the cybernetics of Norbert Wiener. It is unfortunate that the difference between "a mechanical brain" and "a thinking mind" is confused.

The attack made upon sense knowledge is equally an attack upon technical instruments inasmuch as these are aids to the senses in observing the facts of nature. The most powerful telescope is meaningless without the human eye. Apart from man these artifacts are not intelligible. On the other hand, errors associated with the senses arise not in the senses themselves but in false judgments of their data by the mind. Truth and error are in judgment corresponding or not corresponding to reality.

In the method of cosmology the mind ascends from the observation of the sensible facts of nature through the avenues of abstraction to the comprehension of the common properties of mobile beings, and by more intensive abstraction it draws forth the knowledge of mobile being itself from the study of the properties. The human mind does not know essence immediately; essence is not experienced. It is reasoned to from the content of our experience of the sensible manifestations of mobile being.

---

[1] In 2 *Phys.*, lect. 1, n. 8.
[2] In 1 *Phys.*, lect. 2, n. 7.

This demonstration takes place in what the Thomists call the first degree of abstraction.

Abstraction is the act of the human intellect by which it draws from the sensible image of a thing the essential notes, as "rational" and "animal" from the sensible image of man. There are various degrees of abstraction classified according as the mind ascends from the sensible into the intelligible. In the science of cosmology the mind draws forth or abstracts from the individual sensible mobile beings certain common properties and from these it draws out the knowledge of the four cases which constitute the definition of mobile being.

In the first degree of abstraction something is obtained by the mind and something remains untouched. The mind leaves aside the individual matter and fixes its insight on the common sensible matter of the mobile. It abstracts what is common to mobile being and leaves aside the consideration of the individuality of this and that mobile being. As we have already noted regarding cosmology, the object of this abstraction is not a summation of mobilities or a general image of mobile beings, but rather the meaning of the mobile itself. Hence, what is left behind is the individual matter of mobile beings and what is obtained is the intelligibility of being in sensible matter and motion which the Thomists call common sensible matter.

No natural science is simply concerned with the individual. Archimedes in his formulation of the abstract physical law, which applies to the conduct of all solids immersed in liquids and gases, is not concerned with this loofah in his bath, or this piece of ebony sinking in a pool, or the behavior of this ship in the sea. This scientific abstraction formally pertains to the law of flotation as such and not to this or that floating object. So too, Newton's law of gravitation abstracts from individual sensible matter. There is not a law for a falling leaf, another for our undignified collapse on a slippery pavement, and another for our own firm grip on the ground beneath our feet as our planet moves on through space. The one abstract law of gravitation applies to all these individual sensible events. Science is not concerned with individual facts as such.

The concept of mobile being itself transcends individual mobile beings; it pertains to what is common to them all. Furthermore, it surpasses the abstraction of physics, chemistry,

astronomy and other experimental sciences. Although these natural sciences are also in the first degree of abstraction, cosmology exceeds their abstractions since it concerns all mobile beings
simply as mobile. It does not deduce some functional formula
which renders intelligible the motion of a mass of electrons under
certain conditions of research. Its object is to render intelligible
that phase of reality which is in sensible matter and in motion
rather than some class of mobility which is the restricted object
of an experimental science, as atomic physicists study atoms and
botanists study plants. Cosmology is situated on the Olympus of
the first degree of abstraction of common sensible matter.

From the standpoint of abstracting from matter, the mind
can proceed further. In the second degree, in mathematics, the
mind abstracting puts aside not only individual matter of mobile
beings but also their sensible matter. The mathematical formula
(a x b = ab) may refer to atoms or elephants. As a mathematical
formula it connotes a quantitative relationship which is symbolically represented. The individual sensible matter to which it
may refer is not intelligible from the mathematical abstraction
itself although its matter is intelligible quantitatively. In applied
mathematics the intelligibility of mathematical formula calls for
reference to the sensible world. This is worked out by experimentation in which some theoretical formula is tested.

The highest grade of abstraction is achieved in metaphysics:
the third degree of abstraction. In this science the mind leaves
behind all matter and draws out the knowledge of being or
reality itself; what it means "to be." This abstraction transcends
all the kinds of beings and seeks to render intelligible being itself. It embraces the material and spiritual, the finite and infinite, and rests in the intelligibility of reality. Metaphysics was
given its name by Andronicus of Rhodes (First century B.C.) who
was the editor of the works of Aristotle. It means the science that
follows the *Physics*, the philosophy of nature. It goes beyond
sensible matter and investigates reality itself.

The various grades of abstraction have a definite relation to
one another. Cosmology is close to the heights of metaphysics
because it concerns essence and the supreme efficient and final
causes. Whereas the cosmologist ascends inductively from the
sensible manifestations of mobile beings to their common properties and then to their four causes, he is drawn to these heights

by deductions from the heights of metaphysics. He is aided by first principles of being in his insight into the data of sensible experience as he proceeds to conclusions about mobile being as it is mobile.

We shall see that one cannot advance from the properties of quantity and quality to the meaning of corporeal substance without the metaphysical doctrine of substance and accident and the real distinction between these modes of being. Furthermore, one cannot ascend from the common properties of mobile being to the intrinsic causes of prime matter and substantial form without the metaphysical doctrine of potency and act.

This is not the same as saying that cosmology is a special metaphysics. Its principles are not formally metaphysical but they involve metaphysical principles which are applied to mobile being. First principles of thought and reality must be resolved in cosmology. However, cosmological principles are not formally metaphysical because they are not principles of reality itself but rather of mobile reality.

One cannot derive the concept of prime matter or pure potency from the doctrine of potency itself. Prime matter is demonstrated by the inquiry into the nature of mobile being, by observation of the sensible world of change, abstracting its common properties, and finally abstracting pure potency from these, as shall be seen. The metaphysics of potency as such is employed in this demonstration, but it is not the demonstration simply. Aquinas would oppose the identity of cosmology as a branch of metaphysics as he argues:

> Each science considers one phase of being according to a special mode, which is different from that according to which being is viewed by metaphysics.[1]

It is inaccurate to call this science the science of being as mobile. It is not the science of being but rather of mobile being as mobile.

The matter of this method is necessarily drawn from sensible experience in that human knowledge must begin with experience. In contrast to this necessary dependence on sensible experience, cosmology has a relative and contingent dependence upon the experimental sciences. This dependence is called relative because these sciences expand in knowledge from one age.

---

[1] In *De Trin.*, q. 5, a. 1, ad 6.

to another—experimental science is constantly on the march. It is called contingent because it is not necessary but rather expeditious for cosmology to use the other sciences of nature in our scientific age.

The experimental sciences are necessary for the comprehension of the specific properties of mobile being but not its universal properties simply as mobile being. For example, quantity is a common characteristic of mobile being. Astronomy describes the quantitative characteristics of the heavenly bodies in great detail, but the understanding of the fact that mobile being is quantitative is not necessarily derived from the content of astronomy. It is first known from common experience of the mobile in a confused way and refined in cosmology.

The experimental sciences delineate the functions, structures and conditions of mobile beings and these delineations should be employed especially in our scientific age as illustrations in the abstract study of mobile being as mobile. A cosmology which would not improve upon the illustrations used by the Medievals would not be in keeping with the general advance in science. Furthermore, many illustrations used by the Medievals from the alchemy, astronomy, zoology, and other studies of their age have been proved to be false. These errors should be corrected in the light of modern discoveries. For example, the Aristotelian division of the heavens into the perishable and imperishable is no longer tenable. We now know that celestial bodies corrupt as well as terrestrial.

It should be noted that an error of illustration should not be confused with the true principle which is being illustrated—a distinction not maintained by many critics of St. Thomas Aquinas. Some modern thinkers say that the philosophy of nature of the Angelic Doctor is of little importance because it antedates the telescope, and so they argue that St. Thomas could not construct a true cosmology according to modern scientific standards. His errors in astronomy are confused with errors in philosophy. These standards of judgment are determined mainly by some form of positivism, the system that asserts that the only valid method is the empirico-metric method of modern science.

Cooperation between the philosopher and the experimental scientist is necessary not only for the sake of an exchange of knowledge but also in order that they mutually respect the frontiers of their fields. The positivist is responsible for much bad work in modern science in his attempt to absorb all the knowable within the potential of the empirico-metric method. Like the pseudo-aristotelian Caesare Cremonini (?-1631), who would not look through Galileo's telescope, the modern positivist generally will not bother to investigate the claims of Thomistic cosmology on the grounds that it is Thomistic and therefore wrong.

These men attempt to stretch the empirico-metric method of the sciences so that it can render the cosmos itself intelligible in its most fundamental meanings. The words of Plato regarding certain astronomers who attempted to make a philosophy out of astronomy aptly apply to the positivists of our times, "I should say that those who elevate astronomy into philosophy appear to me to make us look downwards and not upwards."[1]

There is no one method for all science. The sciences philosophical, mathematical and experimental are distinguished by their objects and their methods. Their very vocabularies are different. Each science is good within its own limits, but no science has unlimited scope. No one science can monopolize the real; being is too complex. The science with the more universal object as cosmology cannot be explored by such a science as modern physics which has a less universal object, namely, the study of the secondary principles of mobility. This will be made manifest as the real meaning of cosmology is grasped in studying its demonstrations.

Those who tyrannize the sciences by imposing one method for all science commit the fallacy of the uniform method. This fallacy occurs time and again in the history of human thought. It usually accompanies the rise of a new science that is heralded by some enthusiasts as the remedy for all the ills of man. Alexander Pope, the classical English poet, expressed the exaggerated esteem for a great scientist in the couplet:

> *Nature and nature's laws lay hid in night;*
> *God said: "Let Newton be," and all was light.*

Such thinking is very often the fruit of hero-worship or over-specialization, arising in the minds of men who have little or no

---

[1] *Republic,* VII, 529.

training in any discipline but the scientific method which they idolize. It is not uncommon for such trends to end in the rankest scepticism.

The Thomist avoids this error because of his appreciation of the analogy of being and his rejection of monism. His keen analysis of the grades of abstraction reveals his appreciation of the various avenues whereby the mind attains the distinct objects of the sciences that are classified on the scale of being.

In conclusion, therefore, we have noted:

1. Cosmology is the science of the first causes and principles of mobile being.

2. Its subject matter is the mobile beings of the cosmos.

3. Its object is the four causes of mobile being, the material and formal causes, the efficient and final causes.

4. Its method is both deductive and inductive in the first degree of abstraction: the abstraction of common sensible matter in its first first principles. Its method necessarily depends upon sensible experience, and contingently and relatively upon the experimental sciences. The fallacy of the uniform method of the positivists must be guarded against in this study.

II. UTILITY OF COSMOLOGY

The study of facts and techniques in an experimental science is important in the education of a man for work in that field. But the Catholic system of higher education does not stop here; rather, it aims at the higher education of the whole man. Man hungers to know more than the fact and the how of things, he naturally seeks beyond these for the basic meaning of the universe in which he lives.

Cosmology is important because its object is to answer fundamental questions about the universe. Whereas the experimental sciences give only a fragmentary picture of the universe, cosmology goes to the heart of the matter in quest of the ultimate meaning of the beauty and order of the universe itself. It investigates the initial concepts of the experimental sciences, such as the meaning of mobile being, space, time, quantity, quality and cosmic order.

It is unfortunate that the principal occupation of our age is with experimental science and its applications in modern life. The true meaning of nature, the universe in which we live, has become lost to many as they are enrapt in the wonder of man's technological conquest over nature. Human survival, national security, and personal destiny are measured in terms of machines, the instruments of man's genius. Modern man often considers himself the master of his own destiny through experimental science, and his progress is calculated in terms of atomic energy. Our age is certainly the age of "the know how" of technology. But it is not an age of wisdom. It will remain so as long as man refuses to face the nature of things as they are in their being, the reality of the universe in its fundamental principles.

A true philosophy of nature is necessary for a true philosophy of theism, and a true philosophy of theism is essential for the educated man in his search for peace of soul and peace in society. By the light of natural reason the human mind ascends from the visible things of this world to the invisible things of God. The extremes to which man is led by false cosmologies is exemplified in Alfred Whitehead's concept of God as "the harmony of epochal occasions," or by Professor Alexander's idea of God as "a variable quality," and Karl Marx's deification of "autodynamic matter."

The Christian student must be equipped rationally to answer these contemporary errors, and this necessity demands that he know principles of the perennial philosophy. The value of cosmology is, therefore, to be found in the contemplation of the first principles of the universe rather than in the productions of applied science. It is a speculative rather than a practical science. It is a form of wisdom in that it concerns first principles, but it is inferior to the wisdom of metaphysics and the supernatural wisdom of revealed truth, although it is joined to these in the unity of the true.

III. DIVISION OF COSMOLOGY

We have said that the object of cosmology is the four causes of mobile being. We divide cosmology into two parts, accordingly, as these causes may be divided into two classes—namely, the internal and the external. In Part One we study the internal causes of mobile being, that which constitutes its essence: the material cause, prime matter; and the formal cause, substantial form. In Part Two we study the external causes of mobile being: the Supreme Efficient Cause, God, the Creator; and the Ultimate Final Cause, the Glory of God.

Part One is divided into two sections. Inasmuch as we can not examine the essence of mobile being immediately, we must approach this study through the analysis of the prior predicamental accidents, quantity and quality, and the accidents closely allied to them; all these for example, space and place, motion and time, play an important role in our knowledge of the cosmos. These latter subjects comprise Section One. In Section Two we proceed to the synthesis of the foregoing study of mobile being in its predicamental accidents. We demonstrate that the theories of atomism and dynamism do not explain what mobile being is. The doctrine of hylomorphism is shown to give a fundamental insight into the essence of mobile being.

Part Two is also subdivided into two sections. In Section One we are concerned with the origin of the cosmos. Materialism and pantheism are rejected and creationism is demonstrated. In Section Two we treat of the Ultimate Final Cause of the cosmos, the Glory of God. The reality of the purposive finality of mobile beings is proved and the meaning of physical law is analyzed. The possibility of miracles is reconciled with the nature of physical law.

The course concludes with the definition of mobile being in its four causes. This division of cosmology is made in the light of the object of this science to give direction to the student in his study of complex material.

The development of the course through the use of the thesis-method is employed for the sake of clarity and order of thought. The ample use of induction throughout the work is sufficient to show that the procedure is not by sheer formalism, or formal logic applied to the cosmos.

Suggested Reading

Aristotle, "Physics," translated by R. P. Hardie and R. K. Haye, Bk 1, chaps. 1 and 2, in *The Works of Aristotle*, edited by W. D. Ross (Oxford at the Clarendon Press, 1930), Vol. II.

St. Thomas Aquinas, *Commentary on the Physics of Aristotle*, Bk. 1, Lesson 1, translated by R. A. Kocourek (St. Paul: North Central Publishing Co., 1948).

J. Maritain, *The Philosophy of Nature* (New York: Philosophical Library, 1951), pp. 151 and ff.

J. Weisheipl, "The Dignity of Science" in *The Dignity of Science* (Baltimore, Md. Thomist Press, 1961), pp. XVII, XXXIII.

Questions

1. State the real definition of cosmology. Explain what this definition means to you.

2. Define the object of a science. Why is it important to distinguish the subject and object of a science?

3. Is Cosmology the same as General Science? Explain your answer.

4. What does St. Thomas say about the necessity of a science of mobile being in general?

5. Would you say that mobile being as mobile is a reality, or that it is a mere concept of the mind, or that it is a universal concept with a foundation in the finite beings of experience? Explain your reply.

6. Why is the method of cosmology both inductive and deductive?

7. How does the intellect abstract its object in cosmology? Compare this degree of abstraction with the mathematical and metaphysical.

8. How does the cosmological method depend on experimental science?

9. Discuss the fallacy of the uniform method.

10. Write a short essay on the utility of this science to you.

Part One

The Intrinsic Principles of Mobile Being

INTRODUCTION

THE PROBLEM of the intrinsic principles of mobile being is a problem of essence. We seek to penetrate into the inner meaning of mobile being itself. This is a task which requires much labor. It is readily granted that we do not immediately perceive essences. If we did, we could tell without the slightest effort the essence of anything as easily as we can perceive this paper before us. But who can do so? There is no royal road to the knowledge of essences for man in this life.

Essence, or that which makes a thing to be what it is and distinguishes it from other things, is something intangible, invisible, imperceptible to any one of the senses. It is the universal in the singular, the necessary in the contingent, the eternal in the temporal. The senses furnish us with the information about the essence, but another faculty is needed to abstract the essence from the sensory data.

Knowledge begins with the senses but it does not end there. By means of the senses we observe the structures and functions of mobile being. It is the intellect that abstracts the meaning from the sensible data. The intellect compares qualities and judges that they are alike in some ways and different in others; it groups together those which have some qualities or activities in common. By the aid of more extensive observation and judgment the intellect eliminates those qualities and activities which do not belong to a thing but are only there because of some external condition, and retains those that are constant.

The constant characteristics or marks of a mobile being are called properties. They are proper to a mobile being, the signposts that point out to the intellect something beyond them, the inmost reality of mobile being. In the language of the Scholastics, property is any attribute which is necessarily connected with and flowing from the essence although not constituting it. For example, quantity is a property of mobile being. Every mobile being has quantity, but quantity is not the mobile being itself.

When we say that property is connected with essence we do not mean that essence and property are gummed together. They are existing in one complete being. The essence of mobile being is *what mobile being is;* the properties are what it *necessarily has* in the natural order.

In the experimental sciences we are concerned with properties which specify mobile beings according to their proximate principles, e.g., specific gravity, specific heat, and so on. In cosmology our concern is with the most common properties of mobile being in general and not with the specific properties of classes of mobile being. Our formal object, then, in reference to properties is not, for example, the specific quantitative and qualitative properties of hydrogen, but principally the common notes of quantity and quality of mobile being in general.

Although we shall illustrate the universal consideration of the properties of mobile being itself by references to the experimental sciences, our study shall take us beyond the frontiers of the less universal sciences of physics, chemistry, and the other experimental sciences, into the abstract realm of the universal properties of mobile being in general. Hence, we shall treat of quantity itself, quality itself, and the other predicamental accidents.

Section 1

The Accidental Predicaments:
The Common Properties of Mobile Being

EVER since the beginning of speculative thought man has sought to classify the world of real being, the self included, into certain generic concepts to which all other concepts are reduced. In logic the predicaments or categories may be defined as the most generic classes of predicates applicable to an individual subject; in metaphysics they are the ultimate classes of real finite being. It is universally admitted that Aristotle, in the first chapter of the *Organon*, was the first who completely classified the categories.

In the study of categories reference is not primarily made to whether a thing is, but to what its nature and the properties are. St. Augustine appropriately exemplifies these concepts in the following passage:

St Augustine categories

> Wherefore, in speaking of this thing or that, we must not consider what the usage of our language either allows or does not allow, but what clearly appears to be the meaning of the things themselves. When we say he is a man, we denote substance. He, therefore, who says he is not a man enunciates no other kind of predicament, but only denies that. As, therefore, I affirm according to substance in saying that he is a man, so do I deny according to substance in saying he is not a man. And when the question is asked, how large is he? and I say he is quadrupedal, that is four feet in measure, I affirm according to quantity; and he who says he is not quadrupedal, denies according to quantity. I say he is white; I affirm according to quality; if I say he is not white, I deny according to quality. I say he is near; I affirm something according to relation, if I say he is not near, I deny according to relation. I affirm according to position when I say he lies down; I deny according to position when I say he does not lie down. I speak according to condition (habitus) when I say he is armed; I deny according to condition when I say he is unarmed. I affirm according to time when I say he is of yesterday; I deny according to time when I say he is not of yesterday. And when I say he is at Rome I affirm according to place, and I deny according to place when I say he is not at Rome.

I affirm according to the predicament of action when I say he smites; but if I say he does not smite I deny according to action so as to declare he does not so act; and when I say he is smitten I affirm according to the predicament of passion, and I deny according to the same when I say he is not smitten. And in a word there is no kind of predicament according to which we may please to affirm anything without being proved to deny according to the same predicament if we prefix the negative particle.[1]

This classification of the predicaments or categories is not arbitrary but is fully grounded on the various modes of finite beings which are found in the real order. The division of the categories is presented in the following schema:

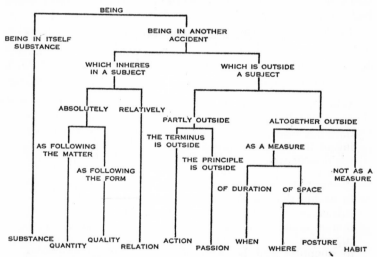

The predicaments or categories are therefore substance and the nine predicamental accidents: quantity, quality, relation, passion, action, when, where, position (situs) and habit. In this section it is our task to study the predicamental accidents of mobile being, especially quantity and quality, in order that we may ascend from the knowledge of these to a knowledge of the first principles of mobile being.

A predicamental accident is defined by St. Thomas as "a thing to the nature of which it is due that it exist in another."[2]

PREDICAMENTAL
ACCIDENT
Def

---

[1] *De Trinitate*, Bk. 5, Ch. 7.
[2] *Quodlib.* 9, q. 3, a. 5, ad 2.

Concerning the predicament of substance, on the other hand, the Angelic Doctor affirms that "it belongs to the quiddity or essence of substance to have existence not in a subject."[1] An accident is a being inherent in another and in such a manner that independently it could not naturally continue in existence. We are all existing in this lecture hall but we do not depend on the hall as a subject of inhesion. We are not accidents of this hall; we are existing substances. On the other hand, the dimensions of this hall could not naturally exist independently of the substances that constitutes the hall itself—the dimensions are accidents.

René Descartes (1596-1650), who is commonly called the Father of Modern Philosophy, rejected the scholastic distinction between substance and accident as a mere verbal expression. We shall consider these and other objections in the theses of this section. It should be noted that the proper meaning of substance and accident is important to cosmology. Otherwise, one confuses the substantial with the accidental or vice versa.

The contemporary philosophers Moritz Schlick and Rudolf Carnap, in their efforts to construct a new philosophy in view of the discoveries of modern science, endeavor to eliminate such concepts as "accident," "substance," and "thing" from their vocabulary.[2] These and other contemporary attempts to ignore metaphysical concepts have resulted in the very verbalism that modern philosophy claims to uproot. Their proponents have become so enrapt in their peculiar vocabularies that it is almost impossible for them to communicate ideas to one another. Scholastic philosophy in general is renowned for its ability to communicate ideas not only from nation to nation but from age to age. The categories taught by Aristotle and in the commentaries on his works by Aquinas are used not only in the lexicon of terms of the scientists but also of the common man.

"Substance," the forbidden word of so many of our contemporary thinkers, is not "the substance" of which St. Thomas speaks but an erroneous concept such as "the substance" of Professor Whitehead who terms it "a chunk of something." These thinkers are rejecting notions they really do not understand.

---

[1] S. Theol., P. 3, q. 77, a.l. ad 2.

[2] M. Schlick, General Theory of Knowledge (Berlin: Springer, 1925). R. Carnap, The Logical Structure of the World (Berlin: Weltkreis-Verlag, 1928).

Consciously they are not negating the common sense notion of substance or the Aristotelico-Thomistic category of "substance." They are far removed from the latter by a peculiar pattern of thought clothed in a vocabulary made to order. These thinkers must be dealt with by first understanding their terms, much as one would deal with a man speaking another language.

Suggested Reading

Aristotle, "Categories," translated by E. M. Edghill, chs. 5-9, *op. cit.*, Vol. 1.

St. Thomas, *On Being and Essence*, translated by A. Maurer (Toronto: Pontifical Institute of Medieval Studies, 1949), pp. 55-59.

H. Renard, *The Philosophy of Being* (Milwaukee: Bruce, 1943), pp. 188-192.

Questions

1. Define essence.
2. How does the intellect arrive at the knowledge of essence?
3. How would you answer the objection: "Positivists are realistic because they deal with tangible facts. Thomists are unrealistic because they concern themselves with intangible essences."
4. What is meant by a property?
5. Discuss the problems of essence and property as they are treated in cosmology.
6. What is meant by a predicament or category?
7. Draw a diagram illustrating the derivation of the categories.
8. Define the predicament "substance" and "predicamental accident." Illustrate the distinction.
9. Is the distinction between substance and accident a case of verbalism? Explain your answer.

CHAPTER I

The Accident of Quantity:
The Static Phase of the Mobile

I. THE MEANING OF QUANTITY

WE BEGIN OUR STUDY of the basic characteristics of mobile being with the analysis of the accident of quantity. In this abstract analysis the student should keep in mind that the subject of our science is mobile being. In this chapter we seek to know the basic static characteristic of the mobile, which we shall see is quantity. We begin with an analysis of this predicamental accident because it is the most important of the predicamental accidents and also because it is commonly confused with substance in modern thought.

The abstract study of quantity in cosmology is not so disassociated from motion that the mind understands it without motion or without matter. As St. Thomas says: "However, the intellect does not so abstract that it understands magnitudes and species to be without matter and motion."[1] The domain of cos-

---

[1] In 3 *Metaph.*, lect. 7.

mology is mobile being, and our discussion of quantity is made only in the light of this mode of being, which is quantified and whose position and pathways in space and time are divisible.

Quantity and quality are considered by Aristotle and St. Thomas Aquinas as the most important of the predicamental accidents of mobile being. Quantity is prior in importance in that all other accidents inhere in a mobile being which is quantified. We speak of the parts of a substance as having a certain quality or occupying a certain place. The other accidents presuppose quantity—although it is true that all the accidents exist together in a substance, there is a definite scale of importance in the role that each accident plays in the service of substance. Quantity is the first in importance among the accidents and this is the real reason why mathematics is so fundamental in the scientific method. The system of inference in physics is set down in mathematical equations. It is only fitting that we should begin our study of mobile being itself by examining the meaning of quantity itself.

Natural bodies are extended in space. They have length, width and depth. They are spread out in three dimensions. The sense of touch most evidently reveals to us the tri-dimensional characteristics of mobile beings. We experience the quantum of our own body, and contact reveals to us the presence of other bodies extended in space which have being distinct from our own. We also experience quantity by degrees, e.g., quantity of heat from a fire.

Furthermore we observe quantity by number—the number of people in this hall. Scientific observation and measurement render our knowledge of quantity more accurate and more refined. Man is now able to extend his techniques for measurement to some of the minute particles of the sub-atomic world. He knows that the electron has a size of about $10-^{13}$ cm. and a mass of .000548 a.m.u.

The quantity of a mobile being is its extension. It has parts outside of parts. We observe that mobile being is not contracted in one point. It has parts spread out in three dimensions in space so that one part is in this part of space and another part is in another part of space. Thus quantity is defined by Aristotle: "that which is divisible into two or more constituent parts of which each is by nature a 'one' and a 'this.' "[1] Quantified being is, therefore, a being that has divisible parts.

These parts are called integral in order to distinguish them from essential parts. *Integral* parts are those that are of the same nature with the whole of which they are parts. Thus the parts of the human body, even though they differ in structure and function, are of the same nature in that they all belong to human nature. *Essential* parts, however, are not of the same nature; they constitute the nature or essence of man, but they themselves are not the same. Thus, as we shall see, prime matter and substantial form are the essential parts of mobile being, and they are radically distinct.

Although we often refer to some integral part as "essential," such as the heart or the brain of man, we are not using the term "essential" in this sense in philosophy. The heart of man is essential to him in that it is necessary for his vital organism. We do not mean that it is an essential part in the same way that prime matter and substantial form constitute essence. Rather we are using "essential" here to connote a necessary integral part of man's organism. It is a property of the subject.

A mobile being has a composite essence as well as a composition of substance and accident. It also has entitative composition, or the composition of essence and existence, which is treated at length in metaphysics. Here it is well to note the various meanings of the term "part," namely, the entitative, essential and integral parts.

Mobile Being	essence { essential parts)	Prime matter Substantial form	Integral parts: e.g. cells, tissues, organs in man; subatomic parts of the atom.
	(entitative parts)		
	existence		

A quantified being is a whole which is actually undivided but capable of being divided into parts. These integral parts cannot be present in the whole as actual; otherwise, we would no longer have the whole but a division. Hence, we speak of the integral parts as potential or capable of division from the whole.

[1] *Metaph.*, Bk. 5, ch. 13.

A being is said to be quantified when it is actually one, a unit, but potentially many. After the division the original whole becomes two or more actual wholes each of which is now a quantified being. Here it is well to note that two things are required for a quantified being: (a) the integral parts into which an original whole can be divided must be present in it before the division; they are there potentially, and (b) these integral parts must be such that once the division is actually made they are single wholes. Before it divides, the amoeba is actually one amoeba but potentially two amoebae. The plant, before slips are cut from it, is actually one but potentially many.

By a "whole" in this context we do not mean a sum, but rather a completely existing thing. The term "whole" is not taken in a merely arithmetical sense but in an entitative sense. When we speak of a part as being potential, we mean potential in the sense that it can be separated from the being in which it inheres and became an actually distinct existing being or aggregate of beings. Thus the electron of an atom is a part of that atom and it is called a potential part in that it can be separated from the actually existing atom in which it inheres, and exist as a "free" electron, no longer as a part of the atom.

A. THESIS I:
Quantity is an Accident Really Distinct
From Corporeal Substance.

1. MEANING OF THE THESIS: We affirm that corporeal substance is naturally found under three dimensions and that quantity is the most important of the accidents of mobile being. We deny that quantity constitutes the essence of corporeal substance.

2. EXPLANATION OF TERMS: Quantity is a property of mobile being. A mobile being is quantified because it has divisible parts.

Accident is a being to which it is due to be in another as in a subject of inherence.

Corporeal substance is that which afterwards will be proved to be constituted from prime matter and substantial form. It is the subject of the integral parts or that in which these parts inhere as the subatomic parts inhere in the substance of the atom.

Really distinct is that distinction which is founded upon reality and not upon a consideration of the mind as the distinction between one man and another. Opposed to this distinction is the logical distinction, a distinction dependent upon the consideration of the mind as is the distinction between a subject and a predicate in a proposition. For example, in the statement, "John is a man," "John" and 'man" are one and the same; mentally, however, "John" as the subject of a proposition is distinct from "a man" which is the predicate. We assert that the distinction between corporeal substance and quantity is not merely logical, but that it is real; that it is founded upon reality and not upon a mental viewpoint.

3. OPPONENTS: When the experimental scientist views mobile being through the techniques of his scientific method, he necessarily sees mobile being according to its parts. The tremendous specialization in science often narrows the scientist's view to a very refined aspect of mobile being in which quantitative factors are isolated and mainly command the attention of the experimentalist. There are thinkers in the history of human thought who have become so engrossed in the importance of the quantitative formulae of mobile being that they have reasoned that quantity is the very substance of this being.

This mode of thought has sometimes been called mathematicism or the doctrine that a body is essentially quantity and that mathematics is, therefore, the supreme science of the cosmos. This mentality was characteristic of the Pythagorean school in ancient Greece. It was revived by the Neo-Platonists, by Roger Bacon under the influence of Arabian philosophy, and among the Parisian nominalists at the end of the Middle Ages. According to René Descartes, the eminent proponent of mathematicism at the beginning of the Modern Era, nature, to be fully intelligible, has to be conceived mathematically as comprising nothing beyond extension and local motion so that everything in the corporeal universe could be represented by clear and distinct images of a mathematical type. This mathematicism, in modified form, remains in vogue in contemporary times.

4. PROOF:

If corporeal substance were not really distinct from quantity, it would follow that corporeal substance could be divided indefinitely into individuals of the same nature.

But corporeal substance cannot be divided indefinitely into individuals of the same nature.

Therefore, corporeal substance is really distinct from quantity.

Major: Quantity, when considered by itself as in mathematics, is capable of indefinite division into individual parts of the same nature. For example, the line AB may be indefinitely divided into smaller quanta of AB. Now, if there is no difference really between quantity and corporeal substance, or a mathematical "body" and a physical body, then what is true of the former must hold for the latter. Therefore, we should be able to divide a physical body indefinitely and still have physical bodies of the same nature as the one with which we started. For example, a plant should be able to be divided indefinitely into plants of the same kind.

Minor: It is a fact both of experience and of experimental science that a corporeal substance cannot be divided indefinitely into individuals of the same nature. Man, animal, plant and mineral cannot be divided indefinitely as a line can be divided. There is a certain quantity demanded by a physical species whether it is organic or inorganic. At a certain point of division under certain conditions the compound is broken up into its elements and elements into their components. Unlike the mathematical "body" the physical body cannot be divided indefinitely into individuals of the same nature.

Why is it that the mathematicist fails to note this difference between the mathematical "body" and the physical body? Of course it is apparent that a mathematicist would not attempt to divide his own body indefinitely in the hope of thereby multiplying the world's supply of mathematicists. The Cartesian would explain the difference between a mathematical body and a physical body by responding that a body as body is indeed extension but physical differences are effected in it through local motion. On the contrary, the new physics has rejected the idea that a body is simply a static block extrinsically pushed about. A body is intrinsically dynamic as well as static as the Thomist asserts.

B. THESIS II:

The Primary Formal Effect of Quantity is the ✳
Actual Extension of Corporeal Substance in Respect to Itself.

The Scholastics of the Middle Ages were keenly interested in the characteristic note of the make-up of quantity. This occupied their minds especially in the theology of the Eucharist. In the Blessed Sacrament the quantity of bread remains without the substance of bread. In the cases of miracles, certain notes of quantity, such as impenetrability, were known to be suspended, as in the case of Our Lord's passing through the sealed tomb at the resurrection. The Scholastics sought to know what note is proper to quantity, what characteristic can not be removed from the accident of quantity and what characteristics can be removed. Such knowledge is of great use to the cosmologist, since quantity is the first of the accidents of mobile being and consequently it is of great service to him in his search for the meaning of mobile being itself.

1. MEANING OF THE THESIS: We do not deny that certain notes of quantity: divisibility, measurability and actual extension in respect to place, are formal effects of quantity. We do deny that any one of them is the primary formal effect. We assert that the primary formal effect of quantity is actual extension of the parts of a body in relation to one another and to the whole.

2. EXPLANATION OF THE TERMS OF THE THESIS: An effect depends on a cause either intrinsically or extrinsically. An extrinsic effect is communicated from without by some agent, as water is an effect generated from oxygen and hydrogen. An intrinsic formal effect is that which is effected in a subject by its form as an inherent determination and so it is not communicated from without. Quantity, as is evident, is a static property and so it does not communicate external effects but it does have internal effects.

The primary formal effect is that which the form confers on a subject primarily and by an absolute necessity. The other formal effects depend upon it. Thus we say that the primary formal effect of quantity is actual extension in respect to itself; namely, the parts of a mobile being in relation to one another and to the whole. This is what quantity primarily and with an absolute necessity confers upon a subject. The secondary formal effects of quantity (actual extension in respect to place, divisibility, measurability and impenetrability) depend upon and presuppose that a substance is itself actually extended.

By *actual extension in respect to place* we mean the parts of a body in relation to place, a certain part in a certain place. *Divisibility* means the separability of the parts of a body from its unity. Mathematical divisibility is the division of a body mathematically considered. It may be carried out indefinitely. We say "indefinitely" because the parts of a body can be divided and subdivided mathematically without coming to a point where further division is unthinkable. The physical divisibility of a mobile being is limited either because of the limitation of the instruments of division, or because a certain minimum of quantity is necessary to a mobile being beyond which it cannot be divided.

Measurability is that secondary effect of quantity whereby a body is capable of being compared with the quantities of other bodies and so it is discerned as greater or less or equal. Yards or meters, pounds or liters—these are familiar terms which pertain to the measurement of bodies. *Impenetrability* is that secondary effect of quantity which prevents another body from occupying a body's place when it is present there itself. The simultaneous location of two or more bodies circumscribed in one and the same place is called compenetration, and it is naturally impossible.

Let us take a simple example. The blackboard in the classroom is quantified. Now the primary formal effect of its quantity is the actual extension of its parts which have a definite relation to one another and to the whole. These parts are intrinsic to the blackboard. It is because of them that the blackboard can be located so that it is said that this part is in this place and all the parts of the whole are in place. Divisibility of the blackboard is only possible because it possesses parts. Measurability is possible because the intrinsic parts of the blackboard can be compared to some numerical standard. Impenetrability or the repugnance of other objects to occupy the place of the blackboard so long as it is here follows because its parts in place exclude the occupation of other objects.

3. OPPONENTS OF THE THESIS: Durandus (?-1332) held that actual extension in relation to place is the primary formal effect of quantity. John Duns Scotus (1265 or 66-1308) affirmed that

divisibility is the primary formal effect of quantity. St. Albert the Great (1193-1280) maintained that measurability is the primary formal effect of quantity.

4. PROOF:

The primary formal effect of quantity is that which quantity necessarily and primarily confers upon corporeal substance and that upon which the secondary formal effects of quantity depend.

But actual extension of the parts of the body in relation to one another and to the whole is that which quantity confers on a substance primarily and necessarily, and that upon which the other formal effects of quantity depend.

Therefore, the primary formal effect of quantity is the actual extension of the parts of a body in relation to one another and to the whole.

Major: Evident from the concept of the primary formal effect of quantity.

Minor: If there were no actual extension in a corporeal substance there would be no quantity. A quantified being primarily signifies a being that has actual extension of parts related to one another and to the whole. This is called by some authors internal extension as opposed to external extension or the relation of the internal parts to other quantified substances. Actual extension is the root of the other quantitative properties. A corporeal substance primarily must be extended itself before it is extended in relation to place and before its parts can be divided from it into separate wholes, before it can be measurable or related to other quanta and before it can be impenetrable in place.

St. Thomas Aquinas affirms: "It is impossible to understand divided parts in matter unless dimensive quantity (actual extension) is first known in matter."[1]

The primary formal effect of quantity cannot be separated from it, but it is not repugnant that the secondary effects of quantity be separated from the essence of quantity. This can be done by God Who has power over the being of things. Thus it is possible to have quantity without local extension or impenetrability or some other secondary formal effect. In the Eucharist the Body of Christ is really present, but there is a

[1] In 7 *Metaph.*, lect. 2.

suspension of local extension in that all its parts are in the same place. The Body of Christ is where the Host is.

II. KINDS OF QUANTITY

Quantity may be divided in various ways. We shall discuss here the main divisions of quantity: the continuous and the discrete.

Continuous quantity is that which is uninterrupted in its being. It is an unbroken expanse, so that its components are united by common limits for example, a line, plane or solid. The components have no limits except those of the whole to which they belong. Thus, the parts of a line have no limits within the line and they are bounded only by the limits of the line itself. The instant any one of these parts is severed by a point, a line or a plane, the continuum is broken. The Thomists maintain that the quantity of a mobile being is continuous; we shall discuss this in the chapter on the substantial compound.

Discrete quantity is quantity which consists of components each of which is an entity itself with its own limits. These components in association form a whole. Its unity is accidental as opposed to a substantial unity because its unity is by association of separate entities, each of which retains its distinct identity. Discrete quantity is twofold: it is *contiguous* if the two or more quantified beings are in contact; it is *separate* if there is an interval between them.

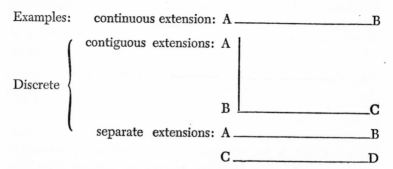

Examples: continuous extension: A _____B

Discrete { contiguous extensions: A | ... B |_____C

separate extensions: A _____B
C _____D

Discrete quantity is quantity actually separated into units or considered as such. This is the domain of number. Discreteness involves the actual separation of continuities or the separability of their potential parts, each of which is considered as a continuum and whose amount is measured by adopting some norm as a measure. Thus by assigning numbers and points in the continuum:

A_____B

we can determine its potential parts as:

A —|—|—|—|—|—|—|—|—|—| B
   1 2 3 4 5 6 7 8 9 10

Such numbers are a type of ordering and measuring of the continuum in its potential parts.

In mathematics we explore a continuum by dividing it, and we number the divisions; this is a kind of conceptual process because what is numbered is actually one. The parts of the continuum are compared with some mathematical standard. This brings us now to the ancient problem of the mystery of the continuum. How is the continuum one and at the same time many? Is there a limit to its divisibility?

III. THE MYSTERY OF THE CONTINUUM

A. THE PROBLEM. A continuous quantity is conceived of as an unbroken extensive whole which is undivided and yet divisible. It is one and yet it is divisible and its divisibility seems to be without limitation. Leibnitz said that the problem of the divisibility of the continuum is a profound mystery. In mathematics it is dealt with in the theory of limits.

B. THESIS III:

The Continuum is not Composed of Indivisible Components but of Components indefinitely Divisible, which are not Acutal but Potential.

1. MEANING OF THE THESIS: We do not deny that in the continuum there are limits which are indivisible, the points which are the termini of the line. We do not deny that the continuum can be physically indivisible either because of the lack of proper instruments or because it cannot be divided further since a certain minimum of quantity is required by a mobile being. We assert, however, that a continuum is composed of components that are potential and indefinitely divisible mathematically.

2. EXPLANATION OF TERMS: The terms have already been defined.

3. OPPONENTS: The Pythagoreans and some mathematicians theorize that a continuum is ultimately composed of parts which are mathematically indivisible. These indivisibles are points; they are devoid of extension. Zeno of Elea (born about 490 B.C.) did not seriously defend the composition of the continuum from indivisibles. He meant to refute the Pythagorean thesis that the continuum is composed of indivisibles by a series of clever reductions to absurdity. Zeno was a monist and opposed the pluralism of the Pythagoreans.[1]

In modern times Suarez and the contemporary Scholastic Gredt hold that the parts of a continuum are formally in act as parts but not as separated individual units since this separation would destroy the continuum.

4. PROOF: *Part 1.*

If a continuum were composed of indivisibles, the continuum would be composed of these indivisibles either as contiguous or as distant.

But each of these is impossible.

Therefore, the continuum is not composed of indivisibles.

Major: Evident. The disjunction is complete.

Minor: Unextended contiguous beings cannot form a continuum because if they touch, they touch mutually according to totality and so they remain unextended. Unextension cannot add up to extension. If they are distant they cannot form a whole which is uninterrupted or continuous.

PROOF: *Part 2.*

The continuum is composed either of indivisible parts or of parts indefinitely divisible.

But the continuum cannot be composed of indivisible parts.

Therefore, the continuum is composed of parts indefinitely divisible.

Major: Evident because the disjunction is complete in our mathematical analysis of the continuum.

Minor: Proved from the proof of the first part.

---

[1] Plato, *Parmen,* 128B.

PROOF: *Part* 3.

The continuum is one being in act.

But the continuum would not be one being in act if its parts were beings in act and not in potency.

Therefore, the parts of a continuum are not beings in act but in potency.

Major: Evident from the definition of a continuum.

Minor: Let us suppose that the parts of the continuum are actual. If this were so, then a continuum would be at the same time actually one and actually many. This is a contradiction.

St. Thomas Aquinas affirms: "Two things which are in act are never one actually, but two things which are in potency are actually one as is evident in the parts of the continuum."[1]

IV. THE MAGNITUDE OF THE COSMOS

The speculative problem of the discrete quantity of the cosmos, a discussion of the magnitude of the cosmos, is in order in this chapter. Is there a limit to the multitude of mobile beings in existence? We know that the tremendous expanse of the heavens exceeds anything that we can actually picture to our minds. At its nearest approach to the earth Venus is 26 million miles distant, and the nearest star, Proxima Centauri, is 25 trillion miles away. The number of stars that can be seen at any time with the unaided eye is only a little over two thousand. With a small telescope one can distinguish about a million stars; with a large telescope at Mount Wilson one can distinguish over a hundred million—all within our galaxy in the universe. This galaxy is a thin disk about 60,000 light years in diameter. It consists of stars and gas. It takes the sun and its retinue of planets about 200,000,000 years to make a trip around the galaxy. Is there an end to the universe itself, namely the total order of mobile beings, or is it actually infinite?

The universe, although of tremendous magnitude, is actually finite. It is well to analyze carefully the terms involved in the problem. The infinite means that which has no limits. Actual infinity in the absolute sense is that greater than which there is none nor can there be in the order of being. Actual infinity

[1] In 7 *Metaph.*, lect. 13.

in the relative sense is that greater than which there is none nor can there be in some line of being, e.g. magnitude. Potential infinity is that which is capable always of receiving a further act. It is also called the indefinite. The continuum is said to be potentially infinite in its mathematical divisibility.

George Cantor (1845-1918), the mathematician, affirmed the non-repugnance of actual infinity. We affirm that no series of quantified beings can be actually infinite.

An actually infinite series is contrary to what is proper to the nature of extension because this would mean an end to the capability of division. But a multitude of bodies is increased by the simple division of any one of them. The positing of the indivisible here would mean the reduction of the extended to a point. But, as we have seen, this is repugnant to extension. Furthermore, to say that the magnitude of the universe is actually infinite is the same as saying that the indeterminate is actual. (As we shall see, the indeterminate in nature is the purely potential and cannot, therefore, be actual as such.) Thus the universe cannot be conceived as an actual infinite. It can be conceived as indefinite.

There is no contradiction, however, in the position that the mathematical infinite is a relative potential infinity. Mathematicians speak of the infinite series, e.g. $1+2+3+4 \ldots +n+$. Such a series can go on without a definite limit because there is potentially always a number greater than any to which we give pre-assigned values, however large. We can never actually conceive of an end of the series.

The theory of the actual infinite is maintained by the followers of the mathematician George Cantor. He was opposed in this theory by the mathematicians Kronecker and Poincare. Metaphysics comes to the aid of the mathematician in his appreciation of the infinite by exploring the various usages of this concept from the standpoint of being.

Among the nineteenth century physicists the theory of infinite space was popular. Einstein's theory offers the notion of the curvature of space and a finite universe. His theory of relativity discards the notion of absolute space and absolute time as proposed by the classical physicists. We shall discuss space and time in the following chapters. We conclude that the universe is actually finite, though conceivable as potentially infinite or indefinite.

Suggested Reading

Aristotle, "Metaphysics" Bk. 5, ch. 13 (translated by W. Ross), *op. cit.*, Vol. VIII; *"Physics,"* (translated by R. Hardie and R. Haye) Bk. 3, chs. 4, 5, 7, *op. cit.*

St. Thomas Aquinas, *Summa Theologica*, P. 1-2, q. 52, a. 1, c.; P. 3, q. 77, a. 2, c.

F. Copleston, *History of Philosophy* (Westminster, Md., Newman Press, 1946) Vol. I, pp. 54-59.

Edward Maziarz. *The Philosophy of Mathematics* (New York, Philosophical Library, 1950) pp. 193-196.

The Concept of Matter edited by E. McMullin (Notre Dame, Ind., Univ. of Notre Dame Press, 1963) pp. 18-27.

Questions

1. What is meant by the predicamental accident of quantity? Explain your answer.

2. What are the kinds of quantity stated in this chapter? How is number related to continuous quantity?

3. State the thesis concerning quantity and corporeal substance. What is the sense of this thesis? Who are its opponents? Prove the thesis.

4. What is meant by a primary formal effect, a secondary formal effect? What is the primary formal effect of quantity? Who are the opponents of this thesis? Prove the thesis.

5. What is the problem of the continuum? State the Thomistic thesis in reply to this problem. In what sense is this thesis to be understood. Who opposes it? Prove the thesis.

6. Write a short essay on the magnitude of the cosmos, demonstrating the contradiction of an actually infinite magnitude of mobile beings.

CHAPTER II

Space and Place

I. THE RELATION OF SPACE AND PLACE TO QUANTITY

THE CONCEPT OF space and place are closely allied to the concept of quantity. Generally, we speak of place as a portion of space and we refer to mobile beings as moving through space. Although we use the ideas of space and place frequently, we do not reflect upon their precise meanings. This is the special task of the philosopher in his search for the meaning of the cosmos of mobile being.

Modern physics employs the concept of space in its measurements. Highly developed mathematical formulae refer to the four-dimensional space-time continuum, but nowhere do we find the physicists defining space-time. The reason for this is that the physicist is not expected to define these basic concepts but rather to use them in measurements. A science of measuring and a science of defining what is being measured are not one and the same thing. It is for the philosopher to define the most basic concepts of nature. In this chapter we shall attempt to comprehend the meaning of the concepts of space and of place and their relation to quantity.

II. THE MEANING OF SPACE

A. THE ORIGIN OF THE CONCEPT OF SPACE

1. Man observes extended mobile beings.

2. He abstracts extension itself.

3. He considers abstract extension as a receptacle for mobile beings for the sake of measuring them in various ways.

Human knowledge about the world begins with the senses. It cannot be reconciled with the "under your hat" philosophy of the idealists. Man does not know about the things of nature unless first of all he senses them. Even the abstract concept of space is established in some way upon the data of the senses. What man experiences is being-in-matter-and-motion manifested in its sensible characteristics. In abstracting the concept of space, the mind makes a certain abstraction from sensible data. It does not consider the hardness nor softness, the color nor the other sensible characteristics of mobile being, but only its extension.

From this consideration the mind builds up the concept of abstract extension independent in itself of the extension of any one mobile being or group of such beings. This abstract extension or limitless spread is conceived as a permeable receptacle which mobile beings occupy and can occupy. It is considered to be a container of an absorbing quality which does not move out of the way of the mobile beings that occupy it. A mobile being is not in space in the same way as a ship is in water, for space is never displaced.

Space serves the human mind for measuring the extension of a mobile being—we say that such a being takes up a certain amount of space or that the space between this mobile being and its neighbor is a certain distance. When we measure mobile beings we are marking off segments, as it were, of abstract extension which is conceived as spread out in all directions as a receptacle for mobile beings to occupy. Space has practical significance to man only in terms of measurement of mobile being, and its real foundation is in the extension of mobile being. Space, then, is abstract extension considered as a receptacle for mobile being.

Let us take for example the simple statement: this room has a floor space of 25x25 feet. We certainly do not mean that space is really containing the floor. The room has a floor surface of 25x25, but not a really existing space. Space is simply a convenient container for marking off the dimensions of the floor. It is an abstract quantitative container. It serves man in measuring areas of distance between mobile beings, and the dimensions of such beings. The architect and the engineer when plotting dimensions suppose an abstract quantitative container in which their dimensions are spread. So, too, the layman in speaking of space conceives of it as a vast container of the objects of experience. The poet imagines it in metaphors as a great hall or chamber in which the denizens of nature move about.

Images of space may vary from person to person, but the basic notion of space is the same for all men: the concept of space as that which bodies occupy and can occupy. We shall analyze this concept and conclude that space is partly real as founded on reality external to the mind and partly logical as produced by the art of the mind. Let us proceed to examine this concept in greater detail in the following thesis.

B. THESIS I

Space is Abstract Extension Considered as a Receptacle
For Mobile Beings; Hence Space itself is a Product of the
Mind but with a Foundation in External Reality.

1. MEANING OF THE THESIS: When we say that space itself is a product of the mind with a foundation in external reality we do not mean that space taken universally is formally in the mind with a foundation in this or that space. Whereas it is true that man as such does not exist but only this or that man, we are not speaking of space itself as formally in the mind in the same way. Space itself, or space considered as a distinct entity, is a product of the mind which is founded upon the real extension of mobile beings and not on individual existing spaces. "Outer space" is really places beyond man's world. "Living space" is really an adequate place for a man to dwell in. We often confuse space and place in common parlance.

2. EXPLANATION OF TERMS: The terms of the thesis have already been defined.

3. OPPONENTS: Some philosophers and scientists believed that space is a purely objective concept. Baruch Spinoza (1632-1677) said that space is simply extension. Sir Isaac Newton (1642-1727) held that space is infinite, that it is the sensorium of God or, in other words, it is through space that God is present in the world.

Others maintained that space is purely subjective. George Berkeley (1685-1753) believed that space is merely the absence of body and so it is purely negative. Immanuel Kant (1724-1804) said that space is an *a priori* condition of external and internal sensation which is imposed by the mind on the data of the senses. The universal and necessary character of space made Kant believe that it is *a priori* because it is a postulate of the Kantian system that nothing necessary and universal can come from experience.

4: PROOF: *Part* 1: Space is abstract extension.

Dimensional expansion considered apart from other properties of mobile being as color, force, resistance, is essential to the concept of space.

But dimensional expansion itself, conceived without the other properties of mobile beings, is abstract extension.

Therefore, space is abstract extension.

PROOF: *Part* 2: The abstract extension of space is considered as a receptacle for mobile beings.

Whatever is considered as being occupied by something or void of it, that in which something is contained and moves, is considered as a receptacle for something.

But we consider the abstract extension of space in relation to mobile beings in this way.

Therefore, the abstract extension of space is considered as a receptacle for mobile beings.

PROOF: *Part* 3: Space *as such* is a product of the mind.

A thing is said to be a product of the mind which is conceived as an existing thing but which in itself cannot exist.

But space as such is conceived as if it were an existing being although in itself it cannot exist.

Therefore, space as such is a product of the mind.

PROOF: *Part* 4: Space is founded on an external reality.

A mental product has a foundation in reality insofar as

there actually exists in the real order something which corresponds to the mental concept.

But the concrete property of the extension of mobile beings is the real foundation for abstract extension considered as a receptacle for mobile beings.

Therefore, space is founded on an external reality.

OBJECTION 1: We say that mobile beings occupy space but they cannot occupy it unless there is something to be occupied.

RESPONSE: We imagine them as occupying something, we concede. We deny that the occupying is real or existing outside the mind. Otherwise, the thing occupied should itself have to occupy space and that occupy another space, and so on *ad infinitum*. This is absurd.

OBJECTION 2: Particular spaces have shapes of their own. Hence they must be real.

RESPONSE: The shape is of the mobile being occupying the space, or that formed by the mobile beings surrounding it.

III. THE KINDS OF SPACE

Space is divided into real space, possible space and absolute space. *Real* space is that which is occupied by a mobile being. It is called real because it is conceived as a permeable receptacle as if coexisting with the mobile being that is said to occupy it. *Possible* space is unoccupied space. For example, the universe could be of greater magnitude, and that into which it would expand is called possible space. *Absolute* space is real and possible space. It is space in its universal meaning. This is not the same as the absolute or infinite space of Newton. The Newtonian concept of space which considers God, Who is purely spiritual, as being present through space is contradictory. Absolute space, as we use the term, has no actual limits because it includes possible space. It is indefinite in that it always admits of addition as the mathematical infinite.

In mathematics space is conceived of in a variety of ways. In geometric space we consider extension itself and do not consider extension as the receptacle for mobile beings. It is not the concept of space which we apply to the mobile beings of the cosmos, but rather it pertains to lines, planes and solids mathematically considered. The type of geometric space which is considered in a geometry will depend upon the postulate upon which it is built. In Euclidean geometry the postulate is, "through any point outside a straight line, only one straight line can be drawn parallel to the given straight line." Lobatchowsky (d. 1856) built up a different system of abstract relations on the following postulate: "Through any point outside a straight line, an infinity of parallels can be drawn to the given line." Riemann (d. 1866) constructed another geometry on the postulate, "Through any point outside a straight line no parallel can be drawn to the given line."

These three geometries are not contradictory. They merely postulate three different conceptual frameworks to which the same real events may be referred. Sometimes it may be more convenient to use the non-Euclidean framework. For example, Einstein used the Riemannian geometry in developing his generalized theory of relativity because it was "a matter of convenience." In 1943, Schroedinger developed another geometrical framework which he claims is more convenient for representing cosmic events since it takes into account electromagnetic phenomena. In comparing these geometries, the words of Poincare should be kept in mind: "One geometry cannot be more true than another, it can only be more convenient."[1]

Some of our contemporaries reject the Thomistic cosmology on the grounds that it was built up on Euclidean geometry. As we have already shown in Chapter One, cosmology does not necessarily depend on scientific data but on the simple facts of sense experience. Thomistic cosmology does not establish the concept of space upon Euclidean space or any other geometric notion of space but ultimately upon the beings in matter and motion.

IV. SPACE AND THE THEORY OF RELATIVITY

Albert Einstein in his work, *Relativity, The Special and General Theory*, wrote, "In the first place, we entirely shun the vague word 'space' of which, we must honestly acknowledge, we cannot form the slightest conception..."[2] In the same work, in his chapter on Minkowski's four-dimensional space, he stated, "And yet there is no more commonplace statement than that the world

[1] H. Poincaré, *Science and Hypothesis,* translated by G. Halsted (New York: Science Press, 1905), p. 66.
[2] A. Einstein, *Relativity, The Special and General Theory* (New York: Hartsdale House, 1947), p. 9.

in which we live is a four dimensional space-time continuum."[1]

How is it that Einstein in Chapter Three is opposed to the use of "the vague word 'space'" and yet in Chapter Seventeen of the same work affirms that the world in which we live is a four-dimensional space-time continuum? The fact of the matter is that in Chapter Three Einstein is speaking of space itself and for him this is a vague concept which, as a physicist, he seeks to shun. In Chapter Seventeen, on the other hand, he is speaking about space in the relative sense as resolved in a space-time continuum described by four numbers: three space coordinates (x, y, z) and a time coordinate (the time value, t.) Time and space must be taken together and not, as in classical mechanics, independently.

Let us take a simple example of the space-time continuum as in the case of the collision of two particles. For the space coordinates we choose three mutually perpendicular axes, say the lines in which the north wall of a room, the east wall and the floor intersect. The coordinates of the point of collision with respect to these axes are x, y, z. T, the time of the collision, is 3.1415 seconds past twelve o'clock. Twelve o'clock is the zero or origin of time. The collision is called a point-event.

In Chapter Seventeen, Einstein is concerned with the measurement of events in space-time frames. The method of physics gives rise to these relative usages of concepts. But is this the same as saying that space, time and other basic concepts of physics cannot be defined? Of course the physicist must shun the attempt to define space and the other universal basic concepts of nature. His method does not have for its object the definition of mobile being and the basic universal concepts allied to it. The concept of space must be vague for a physicist whose task is to use it rather than to define it. The methods of the new physics cannot go everywhere, and if one attempts to stretch them to the very frontiers of the knowledge of nature, then all knowledge must be judged to be as relative and accidental as the measurements of the mobile.

This sort of a philosophy of relativism either claims that only the relativities of measurement are real or else that whatever lies beyond the limits of measurement is unknown to man. Relativism claims that there are no universal truths. Space as a uni-

---

[1] Einstein, *op. cit.*, p. 65.

versal, the relativist argues, is simply unreal, a fiction of the mind.

It is to be conceded that space as such does not exist. But it has some reference to the real world. Although it is not founded on the reality of individual space-frames (as the space occupied by you at the present), it is founded on quantified mobile realities. From this real source quantity is abstracted and conceived by the mind for measuring things in their extension as if they were occupants of that abstract quantum.

The relativist does not explain space as a universal concept; rather he escapes the burden of such an analysis by considering only this or that space-frame. He exaggerates the relative aspect of space by pleading that space is meaningful only in its concrete applications. The Thomist concedes that in any problem of measurement, space is meaningful relative to the frame of reference concerned. Space-frames vary in our mobile universe. But this does not pertain to space itself which is constant in its essential meaning. Relativism attempts to divorce physics, the science of the measurement of mobilities, from the science of mobile being, which explores the most universal concepts of nature. It attempts to ignore the universal in science by reminding us of the obvious: that only the individual exists.

The theory of relativity itself actually shows an absolute or universal feature. Einstein's theory expresses the laws of nature in a form which is the same for all observers, whatever their motions and whatever their systems of measurement. It enables us to isolate certain universal features of the universe which are entirely independent of the observer. For this reason, Einstein's theory of relativity could be called a theory of universal meaning. Many popular errors about the physical theory of relativity would have been avoided, if this fact were taken into consideration.

We must be careful to distinguish the physical theory of relativity from the philosophical doctrine of relativism. The two theories are often falsely identified. The relativity of space in physics is not contradictory to the universal concept of space explored by the Thomist in the philosophy of nature.

V. THE MEANING OF PLACE

The concept of place is closely allied to the concept of space. We locate things by the aid of spatial dimensions. Place and

PLACE) – position of a mobile being in its surrounding
Real term of real motion
Relative accident
determined by 1st immoble surface

COSMOLOGY

space are practically inseparable concepts. At the same time as a mobile being is in place, it is conceived to be in space. Space, as we have seen, is a being of the mind with a foundation in external reality. Place is something real.

A. ANALYSIS OF THE CONCEPT. Man thinks of place as the position of a mobile being in its surroundings. These surroundings contain the mobile being. We locate ourselves in this lecture hall, the hall, in the college, the college in the city, town, or rural area, whatever the case might be. Although we regard place as stationary, we relate it to motion as the term of motion. Without motion which joins two positions, place would not have meaning. Place is a real term of a real motion.

Plural.
in place must be immoble

ARISTOTLE

According to Aristotle, place is the first immobile surface of the surrounding matter. It is "the innermost motionless boundary of what contains."[1] For example, a student is strictly located in this hall by the first or immediate surface of the floor, chair and air surrounding him. This is the real meaning of his place. Commonly we locate a person when we say that he is in the building, in the room or over there by the window. In ordinary affairs we are not concerned with location in its strict limits. But in its real meaning place is defined not in terms of mediate environs but by the immediate containing surface of the matter that surrounds what is being located. In this case of the student his location is determined by the first immobile surface of the air, chair and floor that envelops him.

Although the particles of air are in motion, we speak of the surface of the air as immobile in that the student remains in contact with the same area of the air's surface. So, too, a ship anchored in a harbor is said to be in place even though the water is moving, inasmuch as it is in the same part of the water's surface. This immobility is rendered mathematically accurate by relating the thing in place to fixed axes, a system of coordinates.

B. METHODS OF DESCRIBING LOCATION. The answer to the question "Where is a mobile being located on the earth's surface?" involves the establishment of definite basal directions and the conception of the meaning and measurement of angles. It must have been noted very early in the history of man that the point of the rising sun shifted from day to day, that in the winter

[1] *Physics*, Bk. 4, ch. 4.

the sun rose much farther to the right than in summer. Also, the point at which the sun set did not remain fixed. A general easterly direction could be obtained by observing the extreme points of rising (or setting) and drawing a line from the observer to a point midway between these extremes. The 3:4:5 triangle would then determine the north-south line.

By means of the chronometer and sextant, an instrument for making reasonably accurate astronomical observations, the sailor can determine his location and record it in his log book in terms of latitude and longitude. A complete description of any point on earth will always include the location of that point in terms of latitude and longitude. The poles and the center of the earth are taken as fixed points in measuring the earth's surface and determining location upon it. Whether there is an immobile point or axis in the cosmos in general which could fix the spatial relations of the heavenly bodies, scientists have so far not been able to decide. No definite limits can be set to the extent of the cosmos in the light of man's present knowledge.

The relative immobility of place may be illustrated by a person located in a chair in a moving train. He is truly said to be in place in reference to the train although he is moving with the train. Place is determined by the first immobile surface of the surrounding matter and not by other surfaces of matter near at hand. This relation must be kept in mind. Place, therefore, is a relative accident.

C. The fourfold meaning of presence. We distinguish a four- fold meaning of presence. Circumscriptive presence means that the parts of the mobile being are surrounded by the parts of the containing matter. This is the natural mode of presence of mobile beings. Definitive presence is the presence of a spiritual substance in such a manner that it can only exercise its activity within certain limits of space. The soul of man informs his body. An angel is located where it operates, as the angel that stirred the pool at Bethsaida. The Body of Christ in the Eucharist is in place not through the external contact of the proper dimensions of the Body of Christ itself but through the dimensions of the Host, which remains without the substance of bread. This mode is studied at length in Sacred Theology. Repletive presence is the presence of God in all things. God is in everything by His essence, by His presence in as much as He knows all things, by His power in as much as He conserves all things in existence and concurs with them in their activity. This mode of presence is studied in theodicy.

— a vindication of the justice of God in permitting evil to exist

VI. RETROSPECTION ON QUANTITY AND ITS EFFECTS

As we conclude our study of the predicamental property of quantity, it is well that we briefly review the conclusions reached in this study. Our inquiry took us into a field of new concepts and viewpoints. Whereas in the experimental sciences we speak of the quantity of things in terms of their mass, volume, density and so forth, in cosmology we go beyond these notions to the meaning of quantity itself.

The true student of nature cannot fail to see the value of such a study. Certainly if it is important for man to know the quantitative characteristics of the particular classes of mobile beings, then it is more essential for man to know what quantity is in itself. A system of education which would neglect to define its basic concepts would be sadly inadequate. Unfortunately, this is the fad in our pragmatic age. Quantity and the other accidents of mobile being usually are not studied apart from the method of an experimental science.

Some thinkers have attempted a philosophy of quanta which they conceived as specialists in some particular science. Descartes tried to philosophize about nature by philosophizing mechanics as it was then known. Spinoza attempted to philosophize geometry; Newton, classical physics; and Eddington and Jeans, the new physics. These applications of the fallacy of the uniform method have all resulted in pseudo-cosmologies attempting to build up the structure of reality from accidents without the foundation of substance. The real basis of essence and existence, substance and accident, is neglected by them or only vaguely referred to. An example of this vagary is Whitehead's opinion that substance is a "chunk of something."

These systems are formally mental constructs founded upon suppositions and conjoined by more suppositions that do not tell us about the real world of mobile being, its quantity, quality and other fundamentals. On the contrary, the Thomist analysis begins with the being of the mobile, and so his study of quantity does not begin with Euclidean geometry or Riemannian geometry but rather with the extension of a mobile being. This pre-scientific fact of extended mobile being is the starting point of the abstraction of quantity.

We noted, with Aristotle, that quantity means that which is divisible into two or more constituent parts of which each is by nature a "one" and "a this." Quantity is not the same as the thing quantified. We say that this distinction is not a matter of words, that it has a real meaning. Descartes thought that a body is not a mobile being, but that it is rather extension because for him a body is only intelligible in scientific abstraction as a divisible. This is true when viewed from the platform of mathematical abstraction. But mathematical abstraction does not concern mobile being itself.

In the thesis on the formal effects of quantity we noted especially that divisibility is not the primary note of quantity, nor is measurability. The formulae of the experimental sciences in their atomizing of quantity into its measurable divisions not only fail to grasp what mobile being is, but also what quantity is. They operate on the level of the secondary formal effects of quantity. The primary formal effect of quantity is actual extension, the parts of a mobile being related to one another and to the whole of which they are parts.

In the thesis on the continuum we came upon the problem of how a mobile being can be one and many at the same time. Here we saw that a mobile being although actually one is potentially many. We noted that a continuum is not composed of indivisibles, but of potential divisible parts. These are capable of indefinite division when they are considered mathematically, which is to say when quantity is considered by itself or abstractly. The continuum of a mobile being is really divisible in a definite sense. There are limits to its divisibility. This distinction connotes the real difference between quantity when considered by itself in mathematics and the quantity in a mobile being.

In our study of discrete quantity we found that this is the basis of number. As regards the magnitude of the cosmos of mobile being, we saw that although its extent is very great, it is not capable of actual infinity since this is repugnant to the nature of quantity.

Our examination of the concept of space showed how closely

it is allied to the concept of quantity. We noted especially that space is partly real and partly conceptual in its meaning. The relativity of space, as the term is used in the new physics, is opposed to the "absolute space," of the classical physics or space considered as an independent physical entity. The relativity of space is not opposed to absolute space or the universal meaning of space itself as studied by the Thomist. The concepts of absolute space of the Thomists and Sir Isaac Newton are not the same. The Thomist agrees that space must be taken in relation to mobile being in some reference frame. Finally, in our analysis of place we saw how this concept is related to quantity and why it is necessary to employ mathematics for the precise location of mobile being.

The study of the concept of quantity is highly important in the science of mobile being as such because quantity is the most important of the accidents of mobile beings. We do not know the fundamental causes of mobile being immediately. We must ascend to this knowledge through the avenues of the accidents of mobile being. A seemingly small error regarding the meaning of quantity can lead to a great error at the end of this intellectual pursuit. As we have seen, Descartes never got beyond it in his evaluation of corporeal substance. We shall now turn our attention to the accident that ranks second in importance among the accidents of mobile being—quality.

Suggested Reading

Aristotle, "Physics," Bk. 4, Ch. 4, *op. cit.*

St. Thomas Aquinas, *In 4 Phys.*, lect. 1-9.

J. Maritain, *The Degree of Knowledge,* translated by B. Wall (New York: Scribners, 1938), pp. 201-212.

D. Nys, *Cosmology,* translated by S. Raemers (Milwaukee: Bruce Publishing Company, 1942), Vol. II, pp. 347-398.

Alfred Whitehead, *The Concept of Nature,* (Ann Arbor, Mich., Univ. of Michigan Press, 1959), "Space and Motion," pp. 99-119.

B. Lonergan, *Insight,* (N. Y., Philosophical Library, 1963) "Space and Time." pp. 140-160.

Questions

1. How are the problems of space and place related to the accident of quantity?

2. Explain the origin of the concept of space.

a. Why is it called a logical-real concept?

b. Illustrate what you understand by the space of a mobile being.

3. State the thesis on space.

a. What is the meaning of the thesis?

b. Who are the main opponents of the thesis?

c. Prove the parts of the thesis.

4. Name and define the three kinds of space. Illustrate the first two kinds of space.

5. Critics sometimes argue that the Thomistic concept of space is Euclidean and therefore too restricted for modern usage. What can be said in answer to this criticism?

6. Discuss briefly Einstein's relativity theory of space and the relativist theory that space is only known in its concrete meanings and not in its absolute meaning.

7. Define place according to Aristotle and explain the terms of the definition.

8. Illustrate what you understand by the location of a mobile being.

9. What are the various meanings of presence?

10. Write a short synopsis of your retrospection on quantity and its effects.

CHAPTER III

The Accident of Quality:
The Dynamic Phase of the Mobile

I. THE MEANING OF QUALITY

THE STUDY of quantity and its effects, the subject of the preceding chapters, is the study of the static characteristics of mobile being. In this chapter we shall begin our consideration of the dynamic characteristics of mobile being. The accident of quality answers the question: "what sort of a mobile being?" "*Quale Mobile?*" The physicist answers this problem by analysis of the physical qualities of the mobile in its energies, mechanical, electromagnetic and so forth. The studies of color, sound, magnetism, also pertain to the category of quality. In Cosmology, however, we consider quality itself. What is the meaning of the concept?

Generally speaking, quality means a modification of a being, as when we say that man is two-footed. Qualities dispose the integral parts of a mobile being so that they are in some particular figure, have a given color, manifest a certain resistance and so forth.

St. Thomas distinguishes qualities that are natural to a thing from those that are acquired. In this chapter we are concerned with qualities that are natural to a thing or those that are in a subject in virtue of its nature. We are principally concerned with the natural qualities of a mobile being that are deeply rooted in the being as opposed to what St. Thomas calls "qualities on the surface" such as shape. The Angelic Doctor says of the former:

> As to natural qualities, some regard a thing in the point of its being in a state of potentiality ... while others regard a thing which is in act ...[1]

We shall consider these qualities of the action and passion of a mobile being. Thus, we define the natural qualities rooted in the mobile being as proximate principles of acting and receiving activity.

THESIS V:

Qualities are Intrinsic, Active and Passive,
Proximate Principles of Modifications in Mobile Beings.

1. MEANING OF THE THESIS: We have already explained what we mean by natural qualities of mobile beings. We affirm that there are proximate principles in mobile beings which determine them to act and to receive activity in definite ways. We deny that the action and reaction of mobile beings can be explained by quantities striking against one another or by extension moved about at random.

2. EXPLANATION OF TERMS: A proximate principle is so called in order to distinguish it from the substantial form, which is the first and radical principle of activity in mobile being. An intrinsic proximate principle is within the mobile being, modifying it in a secondary way. Under the term modification in this context we include the transient acts of inanimate mobile beings such as heat, magnetism and electricity. We also include the immanent activities of living mobile being, such as metabolism. A transient activity is one that takes its origin in a mobile being, but its termination is outside the being, as heat of the sun affects something other than the sun heating. An immanent activity is one that arises in the being and has its termination within the same being; for example, the digestive processes in man.

These natural qualities are divided into active and passive. The proximate principle of determining an operation is called

[1] *S. Theol. P.* 1-2, q. 49, a. 2, c.

active, such as the power of one element to attract another. The proximate principle of receiving activity is called passive; such as the quality of iron filings to be acted on by magnetic forces. A quality is usually both active and passive. Figure, however, is only passive. It is determined by the termination of the extended mobile being in some definite manner.

3. OPPONENTS: The mechanists maintain that all that can be said about the modifications in mobile beings can be explained by extension and local motion. Consequently, there are no natural qualities that determine action and passion. The term "mechanism" was given currency as a name for this trend by J. Herbart (1776-1841). René Descartes taught that God communicated motion to the inert masses of matter. This opinion was later abandoned by mechanists and modifications in the mobile were attributed to the chance combination of matter in motion. These neo-mechanists claim that man cannot know the principles of activities but only their space-time relations; they oppose the doctrine of causality. P. Poincaré affirmed, "The true relations between real objects are the only reality we can hope to reach."[1]

4. PROOF:

Mobile beings have uniform and stable modifications.

But these uniform and stable modifications demand that mobile beings have intrinsic, proximate principles of action and reaction.

Therefore, mobile beings have qualities.

Major: It is evident from common experience and natural science that mobile beings have modifications. Man undergoes physical changes from his infancy to youth, to maturity and old age. We note that the qualitative changes in water from a liquid state into ice or steam. Changes occur in figure through condensation and rarefaction. These are among the many physical, mechanical and other modifications noted in mobile beings by common experience and the natural sciences.

Minor: The natural sciences record proper, stable and uniform modifications in mobile beings. These activities cannot be explained adequately by "the chance striking of quantities." They manifest definite tendencies of mobile being in action. The

[1] J. Poincaré, *Science and Hypothesis,* translated by G. Halsted (New York: The Science Press, 1905), p. 100.

chance-impact of particles is indefinitely variable. This indefinite variability cannot explain the uniform and stable activities of mobile beings.

The fixed activities of a mobile being demand definite determinations or qualities in the being by which it acts in a stable and uniform manner. It is absurd to account for water freezing by the mere local motion of its quantity. If water is to be frozen into ice, 80 calories of heat energy must be removed from each gram before freezing is complete. Such alteration of mobile being is dependent upon suitable physical conditions to which the particular qualities of mobile being respond in a definite way. It is not, as the mechanists affirm, the local motion of homogeneous mass nor, as the neo-mechanists contend, a chance meeting of particles.

In modern philosophy the revolt against the existence of quality as a predicamental accident really distinct from quantity dates back to the time of René Descartes, who regarded quantity as the essence of body, and to David Hume who viewed the cosmos as numbers in temporal succession. The mathematical picture of events was taken by these men to be the final report on the knowable. This exaggeration of the category of quantity denies the existence of causality in the cosmos and, therefore, the existence of qualities in mobile being. Such mathematicism may conceive of a dream world in which stones may roll up hill and water freeze at 100° C at standard conditions, because nothing is fixed in terms of principles and causes. Everything is variable. Certainly there is nothing wrong in a mathematician conceptually positing such a possible system, but a system of this kind is not our cosmos of mobile being, the subject of study in cosmology.

II. KINDS OF QUALITY

There are four species of quality: (1) disposition and habit, (2) potency and impotency, (3) passion and sensible qualities. and (4) form and figure. The psychological inclinations of man are called *dispositions* when they are easily affected; when they are difficult to change, they are called *habits*. *Potency* is a strong tendency of a mobile being such as the tendency of a rock to fall. *Impotency* is a weak tendency such as the tendency of a leaf to resist the wind. Potency and impotency in this context are altered only when the nature of a mobile being is itself changed in generation or corruption. For example, a chemical compound retains the potency of its chemical affinity for other specific chemical substances so long as it is uncorrupted. After corruption, however, its elements manifest certain different potencies than the original compound.

Passion is a transient quality such as the pallor of a sick man's countenance. *Sensible quality* (patibilis qualitas) is a quality that is proper or natural to a mobile being as the yellow color of sulphur. Form and figure are really qualities of quantity. *Figure* is shape and *form* is proportion. Form adds proportion to shape. In this context form is to be distinguished from *substantial form*.

The experimental studies of the sensible qualities of mobile being is undertaken in detail by the special sciences of nature, such as physics and chemistry. Whereas in the Middle Ages the philosopher of nature wrote upon these topics, the development of the special sciences of nature in modern times has relieved the philosopher of the detailed inquiry into qualities.

III. RELATION OF QUANTITY AND QUALITY

A. THE QUANTIFYING OF QUALITIES IN A MOBILE BEING. The sensible qualities of a mobile being are extended in it; they are quantified. It should be noted that quantity does not develop into quality; rather these accidents complement one another in mobile being. Quantity is never found in nature without quality or vice versa. Hence, Hegel's theorem, "every quantity if sufficiently increased becomes a quality," is false. Quantitative changes are evident in qualitative changes in a mobile being, but quantity never changes into quality.

Quantity, the first material accident, extends the quality of a substance. A quality may be in the various integral parts of a mobile being while remaining the same quality. Although quantitative characteristics are of capital importance in scientific analysis, it must be noted that such analysis is not purely quantitative. For example, intensification or the change from a lesser to a greater possession of a property (a change to a brighter color, for instance) and remission, or the change from a greater to a lesser possession of property (a change to a fainter color) is a qualitative-quantitative change in a mobile being. As we have already demonstrated, modifications in mobile beings are not explained by static blocks of matter affected by motion at random from without, but by the qualities of their natures.

The mathematical method in experimental science has its place but it should never absorb the role of quality in experimental method. Quantity, which is the object of mathematics, is only one of the categories of finite reality. Professor Northrop in his work entitled *Science and First Principles** writes:

> The attempt of certain modern scientists to supplement the physico-chemical categories with ... mathematical equations when found with structures that present difficulties for the physical theory can produce nothing but nonsense. Such procedure is precisely as ridiculous as that of a pure mathematician who would expect to derail the Twentieth Century limited by attempting the equation for a disembodied switch across its pathway.[1]

Experimental science is concerned primarily with the categories of quantity and quality. The experimentalist can furnish the philosopher with much information in this area of study. The philosopher, on the other hand, can enlighten the experimentalist in the basic meaning of experimental science by his analysis of quantity and quality. The complementary role of quantity and quality is fundamental in the evaluation of the reports on phenomena that are noted by the experimentalist in his physical tests with mathematical calculations.

B. ENERGISM VS. MECHANISM. Modern physicists have rejected the Cartesian mechanism. They no longer consider mobile being to be an inert mass in local motion. The qualitative aspect of physics concentrates upon the study of energy. How can energy be liberated? How can it be controlled? These are the outstanding problems of contemporary physics. Atomic energy has been released by the combined efforts of physicists, chemists, mathematicians and many sorts of engineers, but the indication that energy was there and might be released if suitably manipulated was achieved by the physicists.

The opinion of the mechanists that the atom is unbreakable and that all atoms are of the same nature was proved false by the Cambridge physicist, J. R. Thompson. In 1897 he showed

---

[1] F. Northrop, *Science and First Principles*, (New York: Macmillan Co., 1931), p. 19.

that the so-called unbreakable atom could have fragments chipped off its structure. His experiment led to the conclusion that the atom is made of electrons carrying negative charges of electricity and positive charges distributed in some way then unknown. A clue to the fact that bodies are intrinsically dynamic was already given by Professor Wilhelm Rontgen of Munich in the discovery of X-rays. Henri Becquerel had left some photographic plates near some uranium and had found the plates clouded. The only explanation of this, which eventually proved satisfactory, was that bodies previously thought to be static by nature are intrinsically active; their atoms are changing and loosing energy in the process.

This marked the formulation of new physical theories in the experimental and philosophical sciences of nature. The mechanist concept of essentially inert material being was cast aside. The pendulum swung to the other extreme, to energism, the theory that mobile being is simply energy. Wilhelm Ostwald (1853-1932), an eminent German chemist, claimed that the only substance is energy. Ernst Mach, an Austrian physicist, (d. 1916) denied the existence of substance and held that energy exists without a substratum.

Both mechanism and energism contain some truth. Mobile being has its static and its dynamic aspects. These theories "philosophize" experimental science. They fail to master the being that is mobile and consider only the functions and parts of the being. In the serial development of a physical science emphasis is always given to the latest discoveries of fragments of mobile being. The scientist is tempted to say that now at long last he has come to the heart of the matter. Many scientists, lacking training in the philosophy of nature, try to satisfy their hunger for philosophy by attempting to make a philosophy out of mechanics, or nuclear physics, or any other branch of science in which they specialize.

Thus, the parts and functions of mobile being are taken for the whole, accident is confused with substance, quantity with quality or vice versa. A physical method which is serviceable in a restricted area of science is distorted by attempting to use it in excess. Such scientific intermperance is common in our age. Robert Hutchins, former president of the University of Chicago, remarks:

You will have noticed, too, that it has become a tradition in this country for a natural scientist, after he achieves eminence and leisure, to employ some of both in metaphysical and even theological speculations. Without any particular training in these disciplines and with a healthy contempt for those who have, he proceeds to confuse the public further about the greatest questions that have confronted the human mind.[1]

None would disclaim the importance of atomic scientists in our age. However, it is another matter when experts in this field endeavor to reduce reality to a flux of atomic energies. There is more to the real order than the qualities of energies. The cosmologist of the twentieth century has a definite contribution to modern man in his insistence that atomic power is to be identified in the categories of created reality rather than as reality itself.

Suggested Reading

Aristotle, "Metaphysics," Bk. 5, ch. 14 (translated by W. Ross), op. cit.

St. Thomas Aquinas: S. Theol. P. 1-2, q. 49, a. 2. c.

D. Nys, Cosmology, translated by S. Raemers (Milwaukee: Bruce 1942), Vol. II, pp. 118-128.

A Eddington, The Nature of the Physical World (New York: Macmillan, 1933), pp. 1-20.

N. Dampier, A History of Science (Cambridge: At the University Press, 1943), pp. 382-444.

Questions

1. Define quality. Explain the terms of the definition.
2. Prove that qualities are intrinsic, active and passive proximate principles of modifications in mobile beings. Who are the opponents of this thesis?
3. Discuss briefly the negation of causality and the opposition to quality as an accident of mobile being by the mechanists.
4. What are the kinds of qualities and their meanings according to the medieval Scholastics?
5. Write a short essay on the quantification of qualities.
6. What do you understand by the decline of mechanism and the rise of energism?

---

[1] R. Hutchins, The Higher Learning in America (New Haven: University Press, 1936), p. 104.

CHAPTER IV

Motion and Time

I. ANALYSIS OF MOTION

IN THE preceding chapter we have seen that qualities are intrinsic proximate principles of modifications in mobile being. These modifications are effected through continuous and successive becoming or motion (motus). Time, as we shall see, is a kind of successive motion, which is taken as a measure for other motions.

In the first part of this chapter we consider the nature of successive motion. The object of our study is not the same as that of the physicist. The latter treats of the proximate principles and properties of mobile beings, such as Archimedes' principle of motion: that bodies, when immersed in a liquid or gas, displace the fluid and are then pushed upwards by it with a force equal to the weight of the displaced fluid. The cosmologist studies the initial concept of the physicist, successive motion itself, in the light of first principles.

Our cosmos is vibrant with motion. In the United States we

have a speed of about 700 miles an hour round the polar axis of the earth. We are rushing with the earth at about 70,000 miles an hour along its path round the sun. Furthermore, we have the tremendous speed of nearly 1,000,000 miles an hour due to our motion round the galaxy. The kinds of motion and their measurements are described by the special sciences of nature. But what is motion? What is meant by motion itself?

We clearly distinguish between the conditions of rest and movement in mobile being. To be in movement is a process or transition from an incipient stage, the potency, to a final stage, the act. Potency is a capacity to act, such as the potency to walk. Act is a determination or perfection of a subject, such as the act of walking. When a thing is merely in potency to something, it has not begun to change. When it is actually something, it has ceased to change if it has ever changed. In order that it be in motion it must be neither wholly potential nor wholly actual.

A thing is said to be in motion when it is midway between potency and act, when it is partly in potency and partly in act. It is in the state of the actualizing of the potential. It is partly in the state of the actual because it has received some determination when it is being moved. It is partly in potency because motion is not fully determined to its term to which it tends. There is a determining of the capacity to reach the term. For example, when a man is walking home, he is in potency to being at home and he is gradually actualizing that potency. Motion, therefore, is correctly defined as the act of that which is in potency *as such*.[1]

St. Thomas distinguishes potencies to two different acts: the potency to the completed act, as to be at home for the man walking there and the potency to the imperfect act which is the movement itself. The movement is not a special essence or nature but it is in the process of becoming something; this is the reason for the phrase "as such" in the meaning of motion. Motion is the act of a being in potency inasmuch as it is in potency.

It is certainly not sufficient to say that motion is the actualization of that which is in potency. Motion may have begun toward some term but have stopped along the way and never attained it. The phrase "as such" explains that the potency is being actualized toward some term. This is the formal constituent

[1] In 3 *Phys.*, lect. 2, n. 3.

of motion. It is not a complete being but the way to being, the intermediary between potency and act.

Motion requires a subject, an agent and a transition of the subject from potency to act. It requires a subject that being one thing becomes another. For if the subject actually possessed the perfection to be achieved, it could not be moved. There must be an agent that produces the new actuality in the subject. Finally, there must be the transition from potency to act. This transition is the *ratio* of motion.

Motion considered as a determination from the agent is called *action*, in the patient or receiver of the determination it is called *passion*. The action and the passion depend on the reality of motion. Motion is in the mobile being that is being moved. It is the actualizing of the mobile being which is in potency to the new perfection.

Parmenides the Eleatic (C. 540 B.C.) gave emphasis only to the actual in motion. He failed to see that being is also potential. For him there is only actual being and nothing. Heraclitus of Ephesus (born about 530 B.C.) said there is nothing permanent in the world; for him motion is potentiality. This indeterminism or dynamism, as it is sometimes called, is in vogue in modern thought in such thinkers as George Hegel and Herbert Spencer, and in the opinions of many of our contemporaries, among them Alfred Whitehead and John Dewey. The Communist dialectic of nature also favors this view of the cosmos. These trends of thought fail to grasp the real world in its potentiality and actuality.

It must be noted that the term "motion" is used in different ways. Every motion is a transition from potency to act but this transition is of various kinds in respect to mobile being. Aquinas in his *Commentary on the Physics of Aristotle*, Bk. III, lect. 2, mentions the motion of *increment and diminution, alteration, generation and corruption*, and *local motion*. Motion is noted in the increase and decrease of quality, in qualities as in the changes in color and sound, in the generation of substances such as water from oxygen and hydrogen, in corruption of substances as in the dissolution of a compound and in local motion, the change from one place to another.

Failure to distinguish between the kinds of motion is evidenced in many modern studies of evolution. Alterations in a species are frequently taken for generation of new species. This has resulted from the failure of modern science to respect the distinction between an evolution in quality and an evolution in substance, and the other senses in which evolution from potency to act can be used.

II. TIME, THE MEASURE OF MOTION

A. DEFINITION OF TIME. At first glance it may appear that time is the same as motion. The day seems to be the revolution of the earth on its axis. But a little reflection indicates to us the difference between time and motion. Motion is something that belongs to a mobile being. Time, on the other hand, affects all mobile beings. When we say that a mobile being moves quickly or slowly, we know that we are comparing motion with time. If time varied with motion, as they would have to do if they were the same, we could never say of anything that it moved quickly or slowly. Motion and time are not the same. Time is the measure of motion.

Aristotle defined time as "... the number of movement in respect of the before and after."[1] He calls it "number of movement" because we measure time by numbering the parts of a movement. These parts are not actual but potential because the movement is continuous. It is to be noted that the present as an instant has no parts. It is an indivisible. It refers to the actual existing mobile being not as it was nor as it will be, but as it is. The standard of the measurement of time is taken from local motion, usually from the rotation of the earth on its axis and around the sun. The arbitrary numeration of time is described by clocks which serve as time indicators.

Time is not necessarily bound up with local motion. We may use other changes, such as changes in state of life. For example, one might say: "When I was a student in college, I heard you lecture." However, in order to achieve uniformity man has selected a common standard, which is founded upon the rotation of the earth on its axis and around the sun. Thus we say more accurately: "On January 10, 1965 at 9 A.M., I heard you lecture." Man has built up the notion of time as uniform motion in one direction. We imagine time as something apart by itself.

[1] Aristotle: *Physics*, Bk. 4, ch. 11.

Thus we may think of it as a permanent continuum divisible at a point called the present into the past and the future. The motion upon which it is based, normally the motion of the earth, is of course successive.

B. KINDS OF TIME. Time may be divided into intrinsic and extrinsic time. Intrinsic time is the duration of any particular motion as the thing measured. For example, a runners time for the 100 yards may be given as 10 seconds. The duration of the run is not itself a measure of motion but the thing measured. Extrinsic time, to be considered in the following thesis, is a standard rate of movement used as the measure of the duration of other things. The measure is the earth's motion as, for example, it is indicated by clocks. Lunar time, Martian time world vary from earth time.

We may imagine time as an abstract receptacle of past, present and future events in the corporeal universe. We speak of them as "in time." *Possible* time is time considered as a receptacle of all possible movements which could happen. *Real* time is time considered as the receptacle of all actual movements. It extends from the beginning of motion up to the actual present and it is constantly being increased. *Absolute* time is both real and possible time considered as one. This is the concept of time as such, the subject of our thesis. It is to be distinguished from "the absolute' of Sir Isaac Newton. We shall see the analogy between space and time. Things are contained in space by occupying space; they are contained in time by co-existing with time.

C. THESIS VI:

Time is a Continuous Movement Considered as a Measure of the Duration of Mobile Beings; Time as Such is, Therefore, a Product of the Mind with a Foundation in Mobile Being.

1. MEANING OF THE THESIS: We shall show that time is materially founded on mobile being (e.g., the movement of the earth on its axis and around the sun) although time is formally in the mind's measuring. We assert that the mind assigns parts to the successive motion of the earth as in numbering the time of a year. Hence one can number other successive motions as things related to a measure of time: John was born April 1, 1965.

2. EXPLANATION OF TERMS. The terms of the thesis have already been defined.

3. OPPONENTS: Exaggerated realist views regarding time: Pierre Gassendi (1592-1655) conceived of time as a special sort of being, a certain absolute reality. Isaac Newton, Samuel Clarke (1675-1729) and others identified time with the eternity of God. This is what these men meant by "absolute time."

Exaggerated subjectivist: René Decartes held that time is simply a mode of thought. Immanuel Kant maintained that time is an *a priori* sense form of internal intuition antecedent to all experience. Henri Bergson (1859-1941) believed there is no real duration except in our mental states. He seems to reduce the whole of time to the conscious present.

4. PROOF: *Part* 1: Time is a continuous movement considered as a measure of the duration of other things.

Time is essentially an uninterrupted progression to which other things are referred as co-existent.

But this uninterrupted progression is continuous movement considered as a measure of the duration of other things.

Therefore, time is continuous movement considered as a measure of the duration of other things.

Major: Every part of time, however small, follows another part and that without the slightest break in the course. There is nothing in the corporeal universe which we cannot affirm to be co-existent with some point of time.

Minor: But this uninterrupted progression is continuous movement. Movement expresses change of any kind, but as applied to time it is commonly associated with local motion, that is for man on this planet, the movement of the earth on its axis and around the sun. This is usually the material element of time for man.

The co-existence of things with some length of time is why we say that they are contained in time. We have for example, the events of George Washington's life which co-exist with a definite span of years. It is this span of time that sets them apart and measures them from preceding as well as subsequent events. There is always time to serve as a measure.

PROOF: *Part* 2: Time is a product of the mind.

Time is formally conceived as a measure.

But a measure cannot be formed except by an act of the mind.

Therefore, time is a product of the mind.

Major: Evident from the proof of the first part.

Minor: Measure implies a collection of parts into some unity and also their comparison among themselves. But the collection of the parts of time and their comparison is not an objective phenomenon. It is formally constituted by the work of the mind which collects the elements of time into a unity and compares them as past, present, future. This measure is more accurately established as a numerical series which is applied to events by the mind measuring. The years 1850, 1950 are concepts of the mind measuring. Light years measure outer space events.

Inasmuch as there is no actual numbering, time is imperfectly real.[1] If there were no mind numbering motion on a time scale, there still would be numerability in the before and after of a motion's trajectory, which is the real foundation of time.

PROOF: *Part* 3: Time has a foundation in mobile being.

The motion of mobile being is real and exists independently of the mind.

But the motion of mobile being is the foundation of time.

Therefore, time has a foundation in mobile being.

Major: Motion takes place in the world whether we think about it or not, whether we know about it or not.

Minor: Time is not identical with any mobile being for such a being can stop, start, vary its speed. Time cannot conceivably do these things. Yet we build up our concept of time upon motion. We select one motion as a standard, and we complete the notion of time as a continuous uniform rate of change. Inasmuch as the parts of motion are numerable time is real.

D. TIME AS A LOGICAL CONCEPT. A proper understanding of the logical, real, and the logical-real orders is necessary if we are to evaluate correctly the concept of time. The *logical* or conceptual order cannot exist independently of the mind. There would be no such thing as "January 10" without a mind conceiving. The *real* order exists in the nature of things whether we consider them or not. The position of the earth in its transit about the sun at what we call "January 10" is real. The *logical-real* order of the concept of time, is partly dependent on our mental consideration; namely, the mind measuring and partly dependent on mobile being, such as the earth in motion.

A persistent confusion of the real, logical, and logical-real

---

[1] St. Thomas Aquinas, *In* 4 *Phys.*, lect. 23, n. 5.

orders underlies much present-day thinking on space and time. This is very well evidenced in Bertrand Russell's work, *Human Knowledge: Its Scope and Limits*.[1] Russell now maintains that the world of the physicist, in which there are stars and atoms moving in a uniform time in space, is entirely inferential, logical, the work of the mind.

We can understand the logical-real constitution of time by considering, for example, how we arrive at a perfect unit of time. It is called the sidereal day and it never varies. We take a point (any point on the earth's surface,) draw the meridian north and south through that point, and note when a star passes the meridian. We wait until, as a result of the earth's revolution, it passes the meridian again. The interval between the two transits of the star across the meridian is a sidereal day.

The successive motion that is measured is certainly real. The mind measuring, taking a point, drawing the meridian north and south through that point and using this sphere of reference upon which one can plot motion—this is logical, a mental construct which has a certain real meaning in reference to the star and the earth's surface. In this logical-real order the sidereal day is used as a unit of time by the astronomers.

It is not by the light of the stars that the community as a whole regulates the day. Habits and occupations depend on the sun. The sidereal day, with its 24 hours, has to be expressed in terms of the day with which we are familiar. The solar day, however, is not constant. With the earth revolving in an ellipse around the sun and with the axis of the earth tilted on an angle to the plane of the earth's orbit, the solar day lengthens and shortens during the year. It has been necessary to construct an average day with average hours, which do not follow the solar day and hours in their vagaries. This average day is the basis of what is called mean solar time. It is the uniform time with which clocks are expected to conform.

Not until 1878 did a Scottish Canadian, Sanford Fleming, introduce a plan for dividing the earth by means of 24 meridians, each 15 degrees of longitude apart, and reckoned from Greenwich. Each zone would represent an hour of difference in clock time. According to Greenwich time, the 180th meridian indicates midnight; a day ends, a new day begins. It was in this way that

[1] Bertrand Russell, *Human Knowledge: Its Scope and Limits* (New York: Simon and Schuster, 1948).

the logical-real concept of time, as we know it today, was built up by man.

III. RELATIVITY AND RELATIVISM

Einstein in his work, *Relativity, The Special and General Theory,* speaks of time in Chapter VIII, and in the following chapter on the relativity of simultaneity. Time, for Einstein, involves succession and simultaneity. Phenomena succeed each other in time; the one is before and the other is after. When events occur at the same moment they are said to be simultaneous. Thus Einstein understands by the time of an event:

> ... the reading position of the hands of that one of these clocks which is in the immediate vicinity (in space) of the event. In this manner a time-value is associated with every event which is essentially capable of observation.[1]

The postulate of the constancy of light shows that the concepts of succession and simultaneity have only relative value. When two lights are flashed a mile apart toward an observer who is midway between the two points, and he himself is stationary, he will see them simultaneously, provided that they are flashed at the same moment according to the reading of a clock. If a second observer is traveling on a speeding train parallel to the path of this light, the second observer will meet the ray coming from one point and recede from the ray coming from the other point so that the first ray is shortened towards him and the second ray is lengthened. Consequently he will see the one flash earlier than the other, even if he be midway between the two points.

It follows from this that an event may be simultaneous in respect to one frame of reference but successive to another frame of reference. An observer on earth, one on the sun or on any other star would have his own estimate of a length of time. Each one would be different and each one would be equally right. Every reference system, Einstein concludes, has its own time, and time together with simultaneity and succession becomes meaningless to the physicist unless he knows the reference system to which it applies. This is what Einstein means by the relativity of time.

In ordinary life we do not encounter the problem of measur-

---

[1] A. Einstein, *Relativity, the Special and General Theory,* translated by R. Lawson (New York: Hartsdale House, 1947), p. 28.

ing a body in continual motion; hence simultaneity is not a commonplace problem. But in astronomy and in investigating atomic structure we are faced with the meaning of simultaneity. Let us take a simple illustration of this problem. We say that two points on a body are a foot apart when we can simultaneously apply one end of a foot rule to the one and the other end to the other. But if the body is in motion two observers will arrive at different results in their measurements.

We view the world in a four-dimensional order. The observer locates events according to space-time frames. Eddington in his work, *Space, Time and Gravitation,* writes of the theory of relativity:

> Quantities like length, duration, mass, force, etc., have no absolute significance; their value will depend on the mesh system (space-time frame) to which they are referred. When this fact is realized, the results of modern experiments relating to changes of length of rigid bodies are no longer paradoxical.[1]

The theory of relativity reduces phenomena to relations of certain space-time frames. This method is proper to the viewpoint or specialized object of physics. In this way the Einsteinean theory is serviceable in the development of physics. It must be noted, however, that physics as a science itself has a restricted reference; it does not absorb all the knowable. Whereas it is true to say that the concept of time, the duration of the mobile, is relative as it is studied in physics, it is not true to make the absolute statement that time cannot be analyzed essentially but only relatively. Cosmology studies time as such, time in the absolute sense, or universal time as it is predicable in all its relative references. The method of physics has no right to hunt in this field; attempting it would be to fall into the fallacy of the uniform method.

The pseudo-philosophies of relativism ascribe to all concepts themselves what pertains only to modes of measurement. The relative measurements of space, time and motion are transferred to equate what is knowable so that these concepts are robbed of any value apart from measurement. This is an exaggeration of the mathematical method. The next step is pure subjectivism, as is seen in Bertrand Russell's work on *Human Knowledge, Its*

---

[1] Arthur S. Eddington, *Space, Time and Gravitation* (Cambridge: The University Press 1920), p. 149.

Nature and Scope. All things become absorbed in the mind measuring.

We know from experience that mobile beings have a significance in the objective sense as things *per se*; their being does not depend on the mind measuring. Our analyses show that space and time also have some objective foundations. But the philosophical relativist does not grasp this because he is metaphysically impoverished by his relativism. He is mixed up in a complicated system of real, logical, and logical-real concepts which he cannot adequately identify. Note well that we distinguish relativism, a philosophical doctrine, from relativity, a physical method. It is relativism that stands condemned by sound philosophy. The Thomist does not condemn Einstein's theory of relativity as the Soviet theoreticians did for the past thirty years. The latter only revised their stand in 1951.

Thomistic philosophy properly evaluates distinct orders of concepts. The Thomist avoids on the one hand the exaggerated subjectivist view that time is conceptual and on the other hand, the exaggerated realist view that time is real. St. Thomas Aquinas sums it up in his succinct style:

> Time has a foundation in motion, namely, the before and after of motion itself; but in reference to what is formal in time, namely numeration, it is constituted by the work of the mind numerating.[1]

Time is a relation between the mind numbering and motion which is numerable. It is not purely subjective nor is it purely objective.

IV. ETERNITY, AEVITERNITY, AND TIME

If there were no motion, there would be no time. Again, if there were no mind, there would be no time. Time is a universal condition of all bodies in the universe. This statement refers to absolute time. It should be clear that we are not using the term "absolute time" as the classical physicist uses it. We do not speak of God as existing in time but in eternity; for God's duration is an unending now. He is existing without a beginning and without an end, without change, without a past or a future. Hence Boethius (480-525) declares that the eternity of God is "the complete and simultaneous possession of interminable life."[2]

The separated substances, the angels, do not exist in time

---

[1] St. Thomas Aquinas, *In.* 1 *Sent.,* dist. 19, q. 10, a. 4.
[2] Boethius: *The Consolation of Philosophy,* translated by W. Cooper, (London: Aldine House, 1940), p. 160.

for they have existence apart from the corporeal world. Although they do have a succession in their spiritual activities, we do not speak of them as temporal because they are immortal substantially; we refer to their duration as aeviternity. Time, therefore, strictly applies to the duration of mobile beings. Eternity, aeviternity and time are concepts that concern the duration or the persistence of a being in existence.

V. CONCLUSION OF THE STUDY OF QUALITY AND THE OTHER PREDICAMENTAL ACCIDENTS OF MOBILE BEING

The study of the predicamental accidents of mobile being was undertaken as a prelude to the understanding of the meaning of the substance of mobile being, its origin and destiny. The human intellect cannot immediately grasp hold of the essence of things; rather it must gradually ascend to this profound knowledge through the avenues of the accidents. The student of cosmology is interested in the universal accidents of mobile being as the medium for knowing the first principles of mobile being. To achieve this, he is in search not only of the meaning of the common accidents themselves, as quantity, quality, action, passion, place, time, but also he seeks to integrate the accidents themselves according to their priority in importance. This understanding of a hierarchy among the accidents enables the student of cosmology to simplify his analysis of a complex subject. We have noted especially that quantity and quality are prior to all other common accidents of mobile being.

Quantity gives to substance parts in relation to one another and to the whole. The integral parts of a substance are qualified in figure, color, resistance and so forth. Quantity in a special sense is the root of the secondary static properties of the mobile, namely, its external divisibility, location, impenetrability; it makes measurement possible and it establishes the foundation for the concept of space. Quality, on the other hand, modifies a quantified substance. It is the intrinsic, proximate principle of action and passion in mobile being. Action and passion are both implied in the reality of motion, which is the real foundation of the concept of time. Hence, we refer to quality as the first accident of the dynamic in the mobile.

Quantity and quality are the principal attributes of mobile

being rather than space and time, although space and time are of basic importance to those sciences, where measurement plays a principal role, such as in modern physics. Space and time are dependent upon or presuppose the real accidents of quantity and quality. The student of cosmology is in search of what is fundamental in the real world of mobile being. He cannot be satisfied to stop at the periphery of the space-time outlook.

From the very beginning of modern science the mechanists attempted to elevate quantity and local motion to the dignity of the constitutive principles of the cosmos. According to mechanism, quantity and motion are not avenues toward knowing the first principles of the mobile. The mechanists did not consider a body to be essentially a mobile being. They said that body is not constituted intrinsically of the static and the dynamic. For them body is essentially quantity and it becomes mobile by reason of its association with motion which is communicated from without. The notion of quality as an intrinsic proximate principle of mobile being was forsaken. Motion was attributed to body by reason of some extrinsic cause, a force from without. Body in motion, "matter in process," therefore, would be an accidental composite. The mechanists considered substance and accident a matter of words. They preferred to philosophize with the terminology and method of their mechanics. In their view the cosmologies of Galileo, Kepler, Descartes and all the new masters in natural science had displaced the Aristotelian system entirely.

In our analysis of the predicamental accidents of mobile being we have shown how quantity is really distinct from corporeal substance and how quality is a real accident of mobile being. The Thomistic cosmology does not terminate in the study of accidents; rather it begins there. The role of the accidents, the structural and functional, is not depreciated. These accidents have been adequately identified and will be used in the abstracting of the first principles of mobile being.

The understanding of the true role of the static and the dynamic accidents in the understanding of mobile being is basic to the cosmological method. The philosopher starts with these accidents and he asks the questions: is mobile being simply matter in association with motion, or is the only reality motion and is mobile being autodynamic, or does it demand an extrinsic cause for its origin and what is the nature of such a cause? Is there destiny for mobile being or is there only blind necessity or mere chance in the cosmos? If there is a reason for the cosmos, what can it be?

These are the problems which we shall undertake to answer in the following sections of the course. It is well that the student concentrate on the unity of the course in order that he understand the order of its parts. The comprehension of individual theses in themselves is not sufficient. The various theses are not to be taken as independent principles. They are meaningful to this science only insofar as they are integrated in it in view of the object of the course: the intelligibility of the cosmos of mobile being in its four causes.

Suggested Reading

Aristotle, *Metaphysics,* Bk. 12, ch. 2, *op. cit., Physics,* Bk. 4, ch. 11, *op. cit.*

St. Thomas Aquinas, *Summa Theologica,* P. 1, q. 18, a. 1, c.; P. 1-2, q. 31, a. 2, ad 1; P. 1, q. 10, a. 6, c.; P. 1, q. 10, a. 1, ad 1.

J. Callahan, *Four Views of Time in Ancient Philosophy* (Cambridge: Harvard University Press, 1948).

Albert Einstein, *Relativity, The Special and General Theory,* translated by R. Lawson (New York: Hartsdale House, 1947.)

Bertrand Russell, *The ABC of Relativity* (New York: Harper and Brothers, 1952).

Questions

1. Analyze motion in respect to its essential elements.
2. What errors does the Scholastic analysis of motion avoid?
3. Is time the same as motion? Explain your reply.
4. Define time according to Aristotle. Explain the definition.
5. What are the philosophical divisions of time?
6. Prove the thesis on the nature of time.
7. From the history of chronology show that time is a logical-real concept.
8. Write an essay on Einsteinean relativity and philosophical relativism in reference to time.
9. Compare the concepts of time, aeviternity and eternity.
10. Outline our study of the predicamental accidents of mobile being.

Section 2

The Intrinsic Constitution of Mobile Being:
Prime Matter and Substantial Form

makes it to be what it is

INTRODUCTION

W E NOW proceed from the analysis of the static and
dynamic properties to a knowledge of what constitutes
mobile being in itself. The philosophical mind is not
satisfied with a fragmentary knowledge of its subject: it is driven
further to seek the intrinsic basic principles of mobile being, to
get at the heart of the matter.

The cosmological problem of essence has a universal and
fundamental significance because it pertains to all mobile beings
from the celestial body of the greatest magnitude to the smallest
particle of matter. The restricted viewpoints of the physicist and
the chemist deal with proximate principles of phenomena. The
cosmologist seeks the essential composition of mobile being itself. His task is not to distinguish a species of mobile being within the general class of mobile beings, but rather he labors to
know mobile being as mobile.

The cosmologist's problem of essence is fundamental in that
he seeks to know the whatness, the meaning of mobile being
itself. He is formally interested in its essential composition and
not in a structural and functional composition. Thus he investigates the problem: what makes mobile being to be what it is?
what is its essence or substantial meaning?

The question, "What is corporeal substance?" presumes that
corporeal substance exists. It does not pertain to cosmology to
prove the existence of substance, for this is done in metaphysics.
In modern times, phenomenalists, positivists and relativists
(Hume, Ribot, James, Bergson and others) affirm there is no substratum, no such a reality as substance, but only series of phenomena. Kant speaks of substance as something posited *a priori*
by the mind.

In metaphysics it is demonstrated that accidental changes

in the corporeal world, such as changes in weight, size, and color, ought to inhere in a subject which itself does not need to inhere in another and which we call "substance." Otherwise there would be a chain of dependents always naturally demanding a subject in which to inhere but never inhering. This is a contradiction.

Why is it that this problem of essence has ceased to arrest the attention of contemporary thinkers other than the Scholastic philosophers in general? The answer is given very lucidly by Bertrand Russell in a passage from his work, *The Scientific Outlook*. He writes:

> To the typical modern mind nothing is interesting on account of what it is but only on account of what it may be made to become. The important characteristics of things from this point of view are not their intrinsic qualities but their uses.[1]

The emphasis on utility in terms of the industrial and commercial services that can be derived from natural mobiles to man has shifted the object of research from nature itself to the study of nature in its functional utility to man. This pragmatism is the death of philosophy. Technology has supplanted rather than complemented true scientific inquiry in our time especially in America.

There is a notable rebellion against the dominance of this technological outlook, which seeks only for knowledge for the sake of useful facts, in what Jacques Maritain notes as the recent interest in cosmology, or the philosophy of nature as he prefers to call it according to its true Thomistic name.

> But we must add that today we are witnessing a sort of renaissance of the philosophy of nature. This renaissance parallels the retreat of the positivistic conception of science....
>
> Contemporary science's ideas on mass and energy, the atom, mutations due to radioactivity, the periodical table of elements and the fundamental distinction between the family of elements and that of the solutions and mixtures dispose the mind ... to restore to their full value the Aristotelian notion of nature as the radical principle of

[1] B. Russell, *The Scientific Outlook* (New York: W. Norton and Co., 1931), p. 152.

activity, the notion of substantial mutations, which is the foundation of the hylomorphic theory . . .[1]

Notwithstanding this renaissance, there still prevails in modern thought a failure to grasp nature as it is in its reality or at least to resolve the problem of essence clearly. The first consideration that occupies the minds of the twentieth century student of nature, especially in the higher education in America, is the technological viewpoint. How can the energies of nature be serviceable to man in industry, in commerce, in warfare? The science of nature has been neglected for the arts of production. Although the latter are praiseworthy in the true service of man, it is only when we grasp nature in its essential meaning, its origin and its destiny, that we can objectively speak about nature as serviceable in any true sense.

In this section we shall consider in Chapter One, the inadequate theories of atomism and dynamism, which have been proposed to explain the intrinsic constitution of mobile being. In Chapter Two we shall treat of the Aristotelico-Thomistic solution which is called hylomorphism and which demonstrates a basic insight into the essence of the mobile. In Chapter Two we shall analyze the substantial compound in view of the hylomorphic thesis.

---

[1] J. Maritain, *The Philosophy of Nature,* translated by I. Byrne (New York: Philosophical Library, 1951), pp. 151, 153.

CHAPTER I

The Monistic Doctrines of
Atomism and Dynamism

I. Monism.
    A. Thesis 7: Monism Proposed under any Form
        is Repugnant.
    B. Thesis 8: Philosophical Atomism is to be
        Rejected.
    C. Thesis 9: Philosophical Dynamism is False.
        (The Communist Dialectic of Nature)
II. The Common Error of Atomism and Dynamism.

I. MONISM

SOME PHILOSOPHERS, Spinoza among them, admit the existence of a substance but they deny that substances exist. These philosophers are called monists. Monism is any philosophical tenet that asserts that there exists and can exist only one being, independent, unrelated to any other, the sole constituent being of all apparently different beings and identical with them all.

Among the ancient Greeks the Eleatics were monists. Parmenides in the 6th century B.C. considered the world to be one being without a beginning and without an end. Distinction and multitude are sensory illusions according to his theory.

Modern monists include the following: Baruch Spinoza, who maintained that there is only one substance; Johann Fichte, who affirmed that the ego posits itself and the world is the phenomena of the ego; Ernst Haeckel, who said that nothing exists except matter; and Karl Marx and Friedrich Engels, who believed that the material world is an infinite process, unfolding endlessly in time and space.

Christian Science and Theosophy are contemporary methods (rather than doctrines) which stem from the monistic trends in modern thought. Mary Baker Eddy affirmed that we have no material bodies. We are Spirit, Soul, and not body. All is God. Madame Blavatsky and other Theosophists maintain that all is in one life, one consciousness. The Theosophist movement and the influence of continental subjectivism is evidenced in nineteenth century American thought in the Concord School of Philosophy founded by William Channing. Ralph Waldo Emerson, Theodore Parker, George Ripley and Margaret Fuller were among the more representative members of this school. Emerson in his poem, *The World Soul*, wrote:

> *And what if Trade sow cities*
> *Like shells along the shore,*
> *And thatch with towns the prairie broad*
> *With railways ironed o'er? —*
> *They are but sailing foam-bells*
> *Along Thought's causing stream,*
> *And take their shape and sun-color*
> *From him that sends the dream.*

THESIS II:

Monism Proposed Under any Form is Repugnant.

1. MEANING OF THE THESIS: The thesis asserts that monism in the absolute or mitigated sense as it is taught by any of the monistic schools is false.

2. EXPLANATION OF TERMS: The meaning of monism has been given in the previous section of this chapter. By repugnant we mean repugnant to right reason.

3. OPPONENTS: All who maintain monism in any form. Representatives of these trends have been cited.

4. PROOF:

Reason demonstrates and experience testifies to the objective plurality of mobile beings.

But monism under any form denies the objective plurality of mobile beings.

Therefore, monism under any form proposed is repugnant.

Major: Reason demonstrates that mobile beings are many in species and in number. Although all beings have something in common, they are distinguished by other things. Man, a rational animal, is not the same as a species of animal such as the horse.

The vegetable species that the horse feeds upon is not the same as the horse, nor is the mineral species in the soil the same as the vegetable species that is growing in it. The world revealed to us by our external senses is not a monistic world but a plurality of things. Who can assert that all these things are one and that plurality is an illusion without abandoning reason and experience?

Minor: The denial of the objective plurality of mobile beings is evident in the theories of monism.

In the monistic view of the cosmos there is no real difference between man and ape, between virtue and vice, between living and non-living. All such differences are held to be illusory and in some way really resolved in the one. In the ultimate sense all is one, according to the monistic synthesis of reality. The monist is a person who has gone all out either for the cult of materialism—the belief that all that exists is matter; or the lyricism of idealism—all that exists is the ideal, which of course is the ideal world of the monist. Monism usually involves a pseudo-mysticism which seeks to find in nature an immediate communion with the divine.

The denial of the existence of substances, the identification of substance with quantity or quality as well as the failure to grasp the cosmological method itself, has led to many false theories regarding the ultimate constitution of mobile being. Such systems cannot adequately explain mobile being, its properties and activities. This does not mean, however, that they are constructed purely out of fictions. Rather they are exaggerations of some true reports concerning the nature of corporeal reality. Thus as we shall see, atomism exaggerages the static properties whereas dynamism exaggerates the active properties of mobile being. Such systems cannot adequately explain mobile being, its properties and activities.

Our interest in monism is restricted to the universe in the problem of the intrinsic constitution of mobile being. Thus, although atomism refers to a dualism of matter and motion, it is monistic in that it explains corporeal nature as singularly constituted of one principle, namely, extension to which motion is extrinsically related. This is a mitigated monism, such as is evidenced in Cartesianism. Implicitly, however, these theories contain the germ of absolute monism. E. Gilson has demonstrated in *The Unity of Philosophical Experience* how the Cartesian philosophy evolved into the monism of Spinoza.[1]

We shall proceed according to a process of elimination by first showing the falsities of philosophical atomism and dynamism. We shall then attempt to demonstrate the truth of hylomorphism. The hylosystemism of Albert Mitterer is a certain departure from hylomorphism; we shall evaluate this system last as a theory that to say the least approaches dynamism.

A. THESIS VIII:

Philosophical Atomism is to be Rejected.

1. MEANING OF THE THESIS. Philosophical atomism is to be distinguished from scientific atomism. The Thomist has no quarrel with the chemico-physical theory of atoms. In this thesis we attack philosophical atomism.

2. EXPLANATION OF TERMS: Philosophical atomism is characterized by the basic principles: that matter is essentially homogeneous, and that all material phenomena can be adequately explained by purely mechanical forces. It is to be rejected because it is against reason.

3. OPPONENTS: Leucippus and Democritus (Fifth century B.C.) were pure atomists. They sought to explain all reality on the materialistic basis of atomism. René Descartes, the mechinist, (although he disdains the term "atom") sought to explain all bodies in terms of quantity in local motion and figure. Pierre Gassendi (1592-1656), a materialist, did much to bring atomism into vogue in modern times.

4. PROOF: *Part 1.*

Philosophical atomism holds the theory of homogeneous matter.

But the theory of homogeneous matter cannot explain the specific differences between mobile beings.

Therefore, philosophical atomism cannot explain the specific differences between mobile beings.

Major: This is evident from the statement of the theories of philosophical atomism.

---

[1] E. Gilson, *The Unity of Philosophical Experience* (New York: Scribners Sons, 1937), pp. 186, 187, 206, 211.

Minor: We know from the natural sciences that specifically different mobile beings exist in the universe. Thus we note the specific differences between the organic and inorganic; and between plants, animals and man. A theory of homogeneous matter cannot account for such specific heterogeneity.

Furthermore, if we admit the theory of homogeneous matter, we must endow the beings of the universe with the same natural aptitudes and, therefore, with a basic principle of finality which is the same in all. Such an over-simplified picture of the real world is fictional. The leaves of a plant in seeking light are not moved in the same way and to the same end as a bird seeking material for its nest.

SECOND PROOF:

Philosophical atomism affirms only local motion in mobile beings.

But local motion cannot explain all corporeal motion.

Therefore, philosophical atomism cannot explain all corporeal motion.

Major: Philosophical atomists assert that natural bodies are essentally inert. Inert matter is said to be endowed with local motion which is communicated to it from without.

Minor: It is evident that all material forces are accompanied by local motion. We grant that all the forces of nature produce local motion, but we deny that they produce nothing else but local motion.

The special sciences of nature show that bodies are not intrinsically inert. They have inherent energies. Natural bodies are not simply quantitative, they are also qualitative; they have active principles within them, as we noted in the thesis on quality. For example, in the radioactive physical atoms, alpha and beta particles are ejected with enormous velocities. This is not a case of inert matter.

The reflections of the famous physicist Mach are worthy of note on this subject:

> There is no such thing as a purely mechanical phenomenon. When two bodies communicate velocity to one another, the resultant phenomenon appears at first to be one of movement only (local motion) but certain thermal electrical and magnetic variations are always present which will modify the mechanical effect accordingly. In-

versely, thermal, electrical and mechanical conditions produce movement and so purely mechanical phenomena may be reckoned as mere attractions invented to facilitate the study of the physical world.[1]

Philosophical atomism, or mechanical atomism as it is sometimes called, does not explain the constitution of mobile being. It exaggerates the importance of the quantitative aspects of mobile beings and their local motion.

Philosophical atomism is therefore a pseudo-philosophy of nature. In the history of human thought it marks another attempt to draw a philosophical system out of the science of phenomena. It was greatly in vogue in the last century. As Professor Eddington notes:

> The Victorian physicist felt that he knew just what he was talking about when he used such terms as matter and atoms. Atoms were tiny billiard balls—a crisp statement that was supposed to tell you all about their nature ... But now we realize that science has nothing to say as to the intrinsic nature of the atom. It is like everything else in physics, a schedule of pointer readings ...[2]

The downfall of philosophical atomism leads to new theories concerning the cosmos of mobile being. Eddington and other scientists maintain that it was a death blow to human certitude on the problem of the nature of things. They are now satisfied to speak about phenomena reported in the pointer-readings of the instruments of the new physics. Nature is viewed by them as indeterminate, dynamic, unknown in its intrinsic constitution, phenomena without substratum, shadow without substance. This is a logical consequence, if we admit that the method of the new physics is the only scientific approach to the knowledge of the cosmos.

B. THESIS IX:

Philosophical Dynamism is False.

1. MEANING OF THE THESIS: The Thomist is opposed to the one-sided view that mobile being is ultimately only dynamic. He does not deny that mobile beings have energies or powers. He

---

[1] E. Mach, *The Science of Mechanics*, translated from the second German edition by T. McCormack (Chicago: 1893), p. 478.

[2] A. Eddington, *The Nature of the Physical World* (New York, Macmillan 1933), pp. 257, 259.

denies that unextended forces or energies are the ultimate constitutive principles of mobile beings.

2. EXPLANATION OF TERMS: Philosophical atomism denied the reality of intrinsically active mobile beings. Philosophical dynamism of the last century on the other hand, denied the reality of extended particles and recognized only forces as real. This dynamism asserted: (1) there exists in the world simple elements really unextended, (2) the whole essence of these elements is force, (3) all phenomena are the result of conflict of elementary forces which are only modes of motion. Contemporary dynamism maintains that energy is the ultimate that is known by man in nature.

3. OPPONENTS: Heraclitus (sixth century B.C.), according to Aristotle, asserted that "all things are in motion, nothing is steadfast."[1] In modern times the first great exponent of dynamism was Gottfried Leibnitz (1646-1716), co-founder of the calculus. He set down as his first principle, that the primary entities of mobile beings are simple, unextended and indivisible substances, which he called monads. These monads are not subject to outside influences because monads are simple entities and movement implies change of parts. G. Boscovich, a famous mathematician (1711-1787), applied the theory of unextended entities to the inorganic world alone. He added that these entities are incapable of immediate contact, hence action always takes place at a distance. Carbonelle (1890) introduced into the theory the distinction between ponderable and imponderable matter (ether). Rudolph Lotze, Frederick Paulsen and Edward von Hartmann, toward the end of the last century, endowed these simple entities with life. This sort of philosophy of the cosmos is called hylozoism and considers all matter as living. The philosophy of organism of A. Whitehead of Harvard espoused this view. The philosophical energism of Mach, which we have already discussed, is another modern form of dynamism.

Also listed among the adversaries of this thesis are the proponents of the communist dialectical materialism (or diamat as it is called in abbreviated form) as formulated by Karl Marx and Friedrich Engels in the last century. It may be resolved into the following three basic principles concerning the universe:

---

[1] Aristotle, *De Caelo*, Bk. 3, ch. 1 (translated by J. Stocks,) *op. cit.*, Vol 2

(1) The law of the strife of opposites. All beings are composed of opposing forces. They have the character of changing unity, which is only temporal and relative, while the process of change is absolute. (2) The law of transformation of quantity into quality and vice versa. The changes that occur in nature are not merely quantitative; their accumulation eventually precipitates new qualities in a transition that appears as a sudden leap. (3) The law of negation. The series of quantitative changes is unending. Each stage resolves in a synthesis of contradictions contained in the preceding antithesis. Thus, the strife of opposite elements is synthesized in the compound according to the Marxist. This theory is set forth by Engels in his work, *Anti-Duhring, Dialectics of Nature.*[1]

M. Mitin in his textbook, *Dialectical Materialism,* which is used in Soviet colleges, criticizes what he believes to be the idealism of E. Mach in the latter's energism. The Marxians are attempting to uphold their dynamic materialism against idealism because of their traditional odium for Hegelian idealism. Matter to the Marxist is anything objective and dynamic in the sense of their three laws. As Mitin of the Moscow Philosophical Institute writes:

> In place of the old unchangeable atoms there has appeared a system of moving electrons. Therefore, say the "Machians" matter has disappeared. But actually, more exact principles are replacing primitive physical laws.[2]

Mitin along with other Soviet theoreticians are dedicated to the task of convincing the scientific world that the diamat is the scientific explanation of the cosmos. In America, Giovanni Rossi Lomanitz was the principal Communist Party organizer for scientists.

One must be careful not to classify all physicists of our times as dynamists. In their calculations physicists sometimes treat the particles of matter as reduced to the center of gravity as to a point; they prescind from the material medium in which the forces operate and look only to the effects of energy at some distant point. Actually, such a method does not deny the ex-

---

[1] F. Engels, *Anti-Duhring Dialectics of Nature,* translated by C. Dutt (New York: International Publishers, 1940).

[2] M. Mitin, ed., *Dialectical Materialism* (Moscow: Philosophical Institute of the Communist Academy, 1934), Vol. I, p. 55.

tension of mobile beings. It is simply focusing attention elsewhere.

A physicist may consider the mass of a mobile being of whatever size as if it were concentrated at a point, for instance, the center of gravity. If a physicist is considering the lines of force proceeding from a molecule, the size of the central particle is so minute as to be negligible in certain calculations, and so he may find it convenient to prescind from its volume altogether and treat the lines of force as emanating from a point. Such a conceptual schema gives rise to a language that prescinds from the extended mobile beings and concrete media, although it makes no formal denial of these.

4. PROOF:

FIRST PROOF:

Experience and the natural sciences testify that mobile beings are extended.

But dynamism denies the objective extension of mobile beings.

Therefore, dynamism is to be rejected.

Major: Self-evident.

Minor: Monads posited by Leibniz, the point-forces of Palmieri, and the pure energies described by the energist are understood by them to be simple, immaterial and unextended entities. But unextended beings cannot form extended beings. No being can give what it has not got. Hence, dynamism fails to demonstrate the constitutive principles of the essence of mobile being because it denies the reality of extension, an important property in comprehending mobile being.

SECOND PROOF:

Dynamism asserts that the primary entities of mobility are simply active.

But the principle of primary simply active entities of mobility is without sufficient reason.

Therefore, dynamism is a theory without sufficient reason.

Major: Evident from the exposition of dynamism.

Minor: Either these supposed primary entities act upon one another or they act upon themselves alone. If they act upon one another, the other that receives the action is passive. Hence the primary entities are active and passive. If they act only on themselves then there is no explanation for the relations which science everywhere verifies between the changes of mobile beings. Consequently, if one is to save the theory one must introduce the hypothesis of pre-established harmony, which is to say that God regulates the course of mobile beings as if they act on another but they really do not. This hypothesis is not founded upon the world as it is known by experience and by reason. It is a refusal to face the problem.

C. ACTION AT A DISTANCE. The dynamist admits "action at a distance," that is action without any medium through which the action passes to the patient. Hence, they posit only empty space between their unextended entities. But experimental science rejects as physically impossible the action of a physical force through a total vacuum. If there were "action at a distance" the effect at a distance would be instantaneous. Time, however, is required for sound, light, or other phenomena to travel. If the phenomenon is a wave, it must have a medium. A particle also takes time to move across the gap, and so it is not "action at a distance." Dynamists cannot explain why gravitation diminishes as the distance increases and vice versa. This should not be if "action at a distance," which would be instantaneous, took place.

Furthermore, empty spaces or vacua, which the dynamist posits, are contradictory to motion. Once an initial mover has ceased moving a mobile being, the medium does not rest. It facilitates motion. But a vacuous medium has nothing to facilitate motion. Motion could not be in a vacuum. It violates the principle that whatever is moved is moved by another. We are speaking here about a perfect vacuum and not the so-called "vacuum" spoken of by the physicist as in the experiment of pumping the air out of the bell jar. This latter is not really a case of a vacuum.

II. THE COMMON ERROR OF
ATOMISM AND DYNAMISM

The philosophical evaluation of these errors must distinguish them from the physical theories of the special sciences of nature.

For example, physicists sometimes speak of the photon, light darts of unit energy, as having no mass. Now this must not be taken in the sense that the physicist means a photon is immaterial. Philosophers should not interpret the terms of the physicist strictly. What the physicist means is that the photon has no *rest mass*. Furthermore, mass and matter are not identical as Lucien Matte pointed out when he addressed the Second International Thomistic Congress in Rome in 1936. Although the physicist at times speaks of the photon as having no *rest mass,* this is not the same as saying that it is immaterial and unextended in the strict sense or in the dynamist's sense.

Consider another example; Einstein and Infeld as physicists affirm that "Matter is where the concentration of energy is great; fields where the concentration of energy is small."[1] This descriptive statement is not to be judged as dynamistic in the philosophical sense. It describes energy in terms of great and small; it does not define mobile beings as simply unextended entities.

The confusion between cosmology and the science which is now termed "physics" has led some thinkers to philosophize physics. Thus for the philosophical atomist, matter is inert; for the philosophical dynamist matter is strictly a form of simple energy. If we grant that the method of physics can go everywhere, so to speak, then we will agree that the Cartesian physicist in the seventeenth century had a perfect right to say that matter is essentially inert, just as the dynamist today may assert that matter is a form of simple energy, and we may patiently wait to hear what the physicist of tomorrow will say in view of future hypotheses. After all, if we put our trust in physics for the intelligibility of the cosmos of mobile being, then we must expect an ever-changing story.

The contemporary form of dynamism is a reaction against philosophical atomism, which asserted that bodies are essentially inert. The march of physical science has exploded this latter view particularly in the researches of microphysics. The discovery by Faraday of the laws of electrolysis as demonstrating that for every univalent atom there is an electrical charge (or a multiple thereof for a multivalent atom) laid the ground work for the description of the subatomic world. In 1900, Sir Joseph

---

[1] A. Einstein and Infeld, *The Evolution of Physics* (New York: Simon and Shuster, 1938), p. 257.

Thompson had indentified the electron. In 1918, his pupil, Lord Rutherford had chipped a fragment from the atom and discovered the proton, another particle. In 1932, Sir James Chadwick discovered a third particle which is called a neutron.

Rutherford had reasoned that the atom must consist of a number of negatively charged electrons flying around a central body, the nucleus or core. Now we know that this is true. This tiny core is only one five-thousandth part of the atom in size though it is so dense that it contains nearly all the atom's weight. The positively charged nucleus and the negative electrons attract each other, but the electrons do not join with the nucleus because their speed keeps them moving along their orbits. Experimental science does not pretend to have a complete picture of the atom. It is still discovering subatomic particles: as, positrons, mesotrons and neutrinos.

Some scientists have reacted to these discoveries, which emphasize the dynamic aspects of mobile being, by affirming that energy is the basis of everything. Microphysics has shown that mobile being has multiple dynamic aspects. It has not shown that mobile being is fundamentally simple energy. The mathematical character of microphysics could not touch upon an unquantitative or ultimately simple mode of being even as a probability.

Physics and the other experimental sciences are by nature an ever increasing serial report about events. They never discover the primary constitutive principles that underly the events. Men of science reflecting on some newly discovered serial report may think they have the basic truth of the universe but subsequent reports show that they have been studying only aspects or "events" which lead to further problems of research.

So long as men mistake the serial events for basic truth we will have the philosophical atomists and energists. Physicists will try to be philosophers. Of course it is natural for man to want to know the basic story of the universe. If a man has no formal training in philosophy, he can easily turn to the best tools that he has at hand to attempt to philosophize and for some men the best they have at hand is their physics. But all the physicists in the world with all their equations and all their machines can never put all their serial reports about mobile together and know the primary constitutive principles of mobile being. They do not have the tools, the methods for knowing ultimates. Such attempts must end in scepticism, the theory that *truth* is ever variable.

Physics divides mobile being into a multiplicity of measurements, a logical-real world of calculations. These measurements of integral parts and their functions are not the same as the science of mobile being itself but rather they attempt to tell us how mobile beings act under given conditions. Sciences are distinguished by their formal objects. Physics is restricted to physical measurements of mobile being; it describes its measurements for prediction and control of phenomena but does not render intelligible the meaning of mobile being. Thus to say that physics can offer any knowledge of the intrinsic constitution of mobile being is to say that mobile being is the same as its quantity or its quality. The philosophical atomist and the dynamist are driven to these conclusions because they start with the wrong method in cosmology, the wrong approach to the problem of the meaning of mobility. What seems to be a small error in the beginning becomes a great error at the conclusion.

Suggested Reading

Aristotle, *Metaphysics*, Bk. 1, ch. 3, 4, (translated by W. Ross), *op. cit.*

St. Thomas Aquinas, *In 1 Phys.*, lect. 2, n. 2; *In 8 Meta.*, lect 2.

A. Van Melsen, *From Atomos to Atom* (Pittsburgh: Duquesne University Press, 1952.

J. Maritain, *The Degrees of Knowledge, op. cit.*, pp. 168-170.

L. Foley, *A Critique of the Philosophy of Being of Alfred North Whitehead in the Light of the Principles of St. Thomas Aquinas* (Washington, D. C.: Catholic University Press, 1947).

C. McFadden, *The Philosophy of Communism* (New York: Benziger Bros., 1939).

G. Wetter, *Dialectical Materialism*, tr. from German by P. Heath (N. Y.: F. Praeger, 1958).

Questions

1. What do you understand by the problem of the essence of mobile being?

2. Define monism. Who are some of its eminent proponents? Prove that monism is false?

3. What is atomism? Name some of the adherents of this trend.

4. Prove that atomism fails to explain the constitution of the mobile.

5. What is philosophical dynamism? Who are some of its adherents?

6. Prove that philosophical dynamism fails to explain the constitution of the mobile.

7. What is *Actio in distans?* Is it physically possible? Prove your answer.

8. Write an essay on the genesis of the monistic errors of philosophical atomism and dynamism.

Hylomorphism

I. THE HYLOMORPHIC THESIS

THE PROBLEM WITH which we are confronted is the problem of the primary constitutive principles of mobile being, a problem arising chiefly from the difficulty of reconciling being as stable and determinate with being as dynamic and indeterminate, and of reconciling the state of existence with the state of becoming. We know that mobile beings have inertia and activity, extension and indivisibility, flux and permanence, corruption and the recurrence of their species. What intrinsically causes these opposite properties in the constitution of the mobile?

The philosophical atomists falsely explain that mobile beings

Philosophical atomist - inert
Philosophical dynamists - dynamic
Aristotelian- Thomistic - self form.

HYLOMORPHISM

are essentially inert; they neglect to explain the fact that such beings are intrinsically active. Philosophical dynamists, on the other hand, falsely affirm only a dynamic cosmos; they neglect to account for the inherent passivity of cosmic being. The Aristotelian-Thomistic solution solves the difficulty by making a distinction between the principles of mobile being, between subject and form. It holds that every mobile being has two essential constituent principles: a material or potential subject which is called prime matter and its perfection or act which is called substantial form. This teaching is called hylomorphism and takes into account both the dynamic and static properties of the things of nature. The word *hyle* in Greek means matter and *morphe* means form.

THESIS X:

A Mobile Being is Intrinsically Constituted from a Two-Fold Principle: Prime Matter as Determinable and Substantial Form as Determining.

1. MEANING OF THE THESIS: We assert that the essence of corporeal substance, a mutable entity, is intrinsically and really constituted from a substantial determinable principle which is prime matter, and from a substantial determining principle which is the substantial form.

We assert that these principles are really distinct from each other as act and potency are really distinct in creatures. We assert also that these principles constitute one essence because they are not complete substances but incomplete. They are not existing things but principles of the essence of the mobile being that exists. They mutually complete one another in constituting one substantially complete being.

2. EXPLANATION OF TERMS: "Mobile being" signifies any extended substance endowed with various qualities. "Intrinsically constituted" means essentially and ultimately composed. "From a two-fold principle" has reference to the principles which constitute through their union the essence of a mobile being. They are intrinsic first principles which do not arise from others nor from one another. One such principle, prime matter, is the purely determinable substantial principle in the essence of mobile being. The other such principle is determining substantial form, the first act of matter. Prime matter is called prime to distinguish

it from secondary matter in which accidents inhere. Substantial form is called first act in order to distinguish it from accidental forms, which inhere in the essence of the mobile already constituted.

3 OPPONENTS: Philosophical atomists explain the substance of a mobile being ultimately by a static principle; dynamists explain phenomena ultimately by an active principle.

4. FIRST PROOF:

From the opposition of properties in mobile beings:

Static and dynamic properties in the same mobile being cannot be explained radically unless by the essence of mobile being composed from a substantial static principle and a substantial dynamic principle.

But hylomorphism holds that the essence of mobile being is composed radically from a substantial static principle and a substantial dynamic principle.

Therefore, hylomorphism radically explains static and dynamic properties as found in one and the same mobile being.

Major: Evident from the principle of sufficient reason. Every property is rooted in essence, and if the properties are opposite, the essence must have that by which they can be opposed. We have observed that opposite properties exist in mobile beings, the static and dynamic properties. We have noted that the static properties which we studied under their prior accident of quantity are radically opposed to the dynamic properties which we studied under the prior accident of quality, although they complement one another in mobile being. The essential explanation of these opposite properties must be found in essence composed of the substantially static and dynamic.

Minor: Hylomorphism escapes the oversimplification of philosophical atomism and dynamism. It takes into account the static properties of mobile being which require a substantial static principle—prime matter. On the other hand hylomorphism considers the dynamic properties of mobile being which require a substantial principle of unity and determination, substantial form.

We have noted in the introduction to this chapter that opposite properties, static and dynamic, are found in mobile beings. The essence of mobile being explains intrinsically these static and dynamic properties. We have seen how philosophical atomism fails to explain the dynamic aspect of mobile being, and philosophical dynamism fails to explain the static aspect. Hylomorphism takes into account the experiential and scientific facts of both the static and the dynamic in mobile beings and proceeds in the light of a static-dynamic dualism to comprehend the constitution of mobile being itself.

SECOND PROOF:

From the actual numerical multiplicity of mobile beings:

Animate and inanimate species of mobile beings are actually numerically multiplied.

But animate and inanimate species of mobile beings cannot be actually numerically multiplied unless every mobile being is constituted from prime matter and substantial form.

Therefore, animate and inanimate species of mobile beings are constituted from prime matter and substantial form.

Major: The animate and inanimate species of mobile beings are actually numerically many. Notwithstanding the problem of natural species as it is disputed by experimental scientists all agree that natural species are actually numerically multiplied.

Minor: A natural species of mobile being is one actually in species, and it is numerically many in its individuals. For example, man is one in species as man but many in the individuals of the species as John, Peter, Paul. Now mobile beings cannot be many in the same species unless they are constituted from potency and act in their essence. There must be a potential principle, prime matter, which is the principle of the capability of a species to be multiplied in its individuals. There must be an actual determining principle, substantial form, which causes mobile beings to belong to one of the natural species.

Hylomorphism is confirmed by the doctrine of St. Thomas Aquinas in his *Commentary on the First and Second Book of the Physics of Aristotle*, in his *Commentaries on the Seventh and Eighth Books of Aristotle's Metaphysics*, and in his *Commentaries on the First and Second Books Concerning Generation*.

A. THE UNICITY OF THE HYLOMORPHIC THESIS. The hylomorphic thesis provides us with the constitutive principles of mobile being, prime matter and substantial form. We shall now proceed to examine these principles in themselves. It must be noted, however, that the hylomorphic thesis cannot be demonstrated on the empirical level. It cannot be proved by experimentation and mathematical calculation. It is a philosophical thesis in the strict sense. Such knowledge is necessarily very universal and general, but by reason of its very universality and nearness to the supreme principles of thought and being, it possesses a degree of certitude superior to that knowledge which deals only with the sensible properties of things.

The student must realize the unique character of the object and method of the grade of abstraction that he is using in this philosophical problem in cosmology. On the one hand, he should note that the hylomorphic principles are not metaphysical such as potency and act; they are not principles devoid of matter and predicable of being as being. They are the intrinsic principles of mobile being as mobile.

Furthermore, although prime matter and substantial form essentially constitute beings in sensible matter, these principles are not themselves sensible. They are not subject to experimental tests, nor are they intelligible in the sense of a mathematical demonstration. Prime matter and substantial form are not sensible in themselves because they are the principles that constitute sensible matter. If they were sensible, as for example, the integral parts of the human body, or the spectra emitted from an element, they could not be the intrinsic principles from which and in which sensible matter itself is constituted. They could not explain sensible matter itself as intrinsic causal principles because they would also be the sensible matter.

B. Hylomorphism is undemonstrable by the methods of the experimentalist. The modern mind often considers the insensible to be unreal. This fallacy has given great popularity to those cosmologies which seek to explain the cosmos only by sensible principles in second matter—the realism of facts. Such thinking will prevail so long as one fails to grasp the kind of problem he is considering: namely, the problem of the material and formal causes of mobile being in its universal and fundamental significance. Such a problem can be answered only by principles that constitute common sensible matter, that make it to be what it is.

Prime matter and substantial form are foreign to the ter-

minology and technique of the experimental scientist in search
of an explanation of the secondary principles of the mobile,
such as the meaning of gravity. This latter is a problem of physics.
The intrinsic principles of mobile being as mobile are intelligible
in their own order. Whereas truth is one, it must be noted from
metaphysics that truth as being is analogous. The experimental
scientist who would expect to solve the problem of the nature
of things in the experimental order of science is like a chemist
who would attempt to dissolve water into its elementary components with the aid of a scalpel. Each science has its own object and method to know truth as it pertains to the sphere of
the knowable of a certain science.

THESIS XI:

*Prime Matter and Material Substantial Form of Mobile
Being cannot Exist Separately.*

1. MEANING OF THE THESIS: We say that prime matter and material substantial form of a mobile being cannot exist separately.
In other words neither of them can have its own proper existence.
Prime matter and material substantial form are intrinsic principles of the mobile being which essentially results from them
and which is the existing thing. Although prime matter and
material substantial form belong to a mobile being, neither of
them may be said to be that which exists.

2. EXPLANATION OF TERMS: Prime matter is the subject from
which that which exists in sensible matter and motion is intrinsically constituted in essence. Material substantial form is
the perfection or act in which the existing mobile being is intrinsically constituted in essence. This substantial form is called
material because such a substantial form intrinsically depends
on matter, as the substantial form of a plant or a mineral. It is
opposed to an immaterial substantial form, as the soul of man,
which can exist apart from matter.

3. PROOF: *Part* 1:

　　To assert that prime matter is in act without substantial
form is to assert a contradiction.
　　Existence is the ultimate act and ultimate terminus of being.
　　But the ultimate terminus of being is fitting only to a thing
substantially complete and terminated.

Therefore, existence is fitting only to a thing substantially complete and terminated.

If prime matter would have its own proper existence, it would be substantially terminated and consequently together with substantial form it could not constitute the substance of a mobile being. Such a union would be an accidental union of two completed substances.

Prime matter is neither a complete nature nor an actual principle of nature since it is defined as a pure capacity for receiving form. It follows, therefore, that we cannot consistently maintain that prime matter has any existence of its own.

PROOF: *Part 2*:

To assert that material substantial form has its own existence is to assert a contradiction.

Material substantial form is the principle determining prime matter and depends intrinsically on matter.

But the principle determining matter on which it intrinsically depends cannot have its own proper existence.

Therefore, material substantial form cannot have its own proper existence.

Major: Action follows being (*agere sequitur esse*). Material substantial form in all its operations intrinsically depends on matter. It has no actions strictly immaterial or spiritual such as knowing or willing. All the phenomena of natural bodies exhibit an intrinsic dependence on matter.

Minor: What intrinsically depends on matter does not have its own proper existence but subsists united with matter.

Principles which do not themselves exist naturally appear to be strange, and one is apt to think of such things as mere concepts with no real foundation outside the mind. However, when the student carefully defines the terms he is using it becomes evident that he is not dealing with fictional concepts. Prime matter and material substantial form are real principles even though they do not exist of themselves because their reality is in the mobile being that exists and which they compose.

The prime matter and the material substantial form of mobile being constitute its essence; essence is not existence in any created being. Thus to consider the essence of the mobile by itself in its constituents is to consider principles which are not existing by themselves but which can have existence only in the actual mobile being. Prime matter and substantial form are non-existents by themselves; they share in the being that exists as intrinsic causal principles.

A. PRIME MATTER. Aristotle gives both a negative and positive delineation of prime matter. These cannot be taken strictly as definitions because prime matter is an incomplete being. Considered in itself, it is formless and has neither a genus nor a *differentia*; both of which are demanded for a definition. Aristotle gives the following negative description of prime matter: "Prime matter is not a particular thing, nor the quality of a thing, nor its quantity, nor is it assigned to any of the other categories which render being determinate."[1] This means that prime matter has not of itself a determinate essence and that it is not in the genus of quantity or in any other genus.

According to Aristotle prime matter considered positively is the first subject of which a thing is made, and not in an accidental manner. The term "subject" excludes the formal cause which is not a subject but the determination which is added to a subject. "First" excludes second matter, the substance that supports accidents. "Of which a thing is made" excludes other causes, for prime matter is the material cause (that from which a thing is made). It is not the efficient cause, that by which a thing is made. It is not the final cause, that on account of which a thing is made.

"Not in an accidental manner"—this simply means that prime matter is not privation, for privation does not enter into the composition of a thing but rather signifies the absence of the form to which it is tending. Prime matter, substantial form, and privation are, as we shall see, principles of generation. Privation always presupposes form and it is for this reason that we cannot speak of prime matter which of itself is formless as being a privation.

Since prime matter is the first substantial principle from which every mobile being is made in its essence, it cannot be produced from another subject but only from nothing. But production from nothing is creation. Since prime matter cannot exist by itself, we speak of it as con-created. It is created with substantial form.

---

[1] *Metaph.* Bk. 7, ch. 3.

It is metaphysically impossible for matter to be known apart from form because the intellect knows a thing through its form, its determination. Hence, our knowledge of first matter is only derived from the union of prime matter and substantial form. Samuel Butler (1612-1680) in the first canto of *Hudibras* makes sport of "the philosopher" who claimed to have seen first matter:

> He had first matter seen undressed;
> He took her naked all alone,
> Before one rag of form was on.

B. SUBSTANTIAL FORM. Form in its widest meaning is that by which a thing is what it is and not something else. For example, the form of man is proper to the human being alone. It is the "rational animal" that sets man apart from all else in creation. For this reason form is called act because it constitutes and determines a thing in a certain mode of being, just as matter is called potency because of itself it is indifferent to any particular mode of being. The matter is the common element that remains while forms appear and disappear in changeable being.

We are dealing here with substantial form which is the determining principle in the constitution of mobile being. It is distinguished from accidental form, which is added to a thing that is already constituted in its substantial being such as the accidental forms of color, weight and shape.

Substantial form is properly defined as the first act of prime matter. It is called "act" because it is the determining principle in a mobile being and to distinguish it from prime matter, the determinable principle. It is called "first" to distinguish it as an act from the act of existence, the ultimate act of being added to essence, and also to distinguish it from accidental forms which are only secondary acts that presuppose substantial act. It is called the act of first matter to distinguish it from the forms of angels which are not received in matter.

Substantial form is the principle of specification, of being, and the first principle of operation. It is the principle of specification because it determines prime matter and constitutes the substance of mobile being in a species. It is the principle of being because by the mediation of form corporeal substance becomes the proper subject of existence. And it is the first principle of operation because action follows being, and a thing operates inasmuch as it is in act. But substantial form is the first act of the substance, of mobile being and is, therefore, the first and radical principle of operation.

Substantial form is material and immaterial or spiritual. It is called material when it depends on matter intrinsically in its being and operation. It must be received into matter in order to exist, as the substantial form of a mineral or a plant or an animal. Immaterial substantial form is form which, although it exists in matter, can exist apart from matter. The human soul is such a form. It is intrinsically independent of matter. It is also extrinsically dependent on matter, inasmuch as its animal and vegetative functions need matter to operate, but the human soul itself does not need to be received into matter to exist. It is spiritual in its nature. Thus, the human soul endures after the death of the body. This is discussed in rational psychology.

III. THE ORIGIN OF MATERIAL
SUBSTANTIAL FORMS AND EVOLUTION

The problem of the origin of material substantial forms concerns the eduction of these forms. From whence do they arise? To the Medieval this would concern the generation of ashes from the burning of wood, as the corruption of one substance gives rise to the generation of another. Or again, the generation of seeds from the plant. The seed must be in some way in the matter of the parent plant before generation. But what is the mode of such being in matter?

It is not correct to say that this problem no longer exists for modern man because of the analysis effected by modern laboratory techniques. The fact, for example, that we now know that water is a compound of the elements of hydrogen and oxygen does not answer the question: how do these elements exist in the substance of water? Experimental science stops at the quantitative-qualitative analysis of mobile being. It does not investigate the problems of material substantial forms as such.

The problem of the evolution of the species is allied to this problem of the eduction of material substantial forms. Contemporary theories of evolution are satisfied to speculate about the evolution of the species without exploring adequately what they mean by a species. Species involve more than quantitative-qualitative relations and consequently their evolution must imply principles beyond the realm of the accidents of functions and structures. It concerns the very principle of the specification of matter, which is in the material substantial form and the principle of potentiality, prime matter.

For the materialist this problem is minimized because for him there is only the material cause. As St. Thomas says:

> For since they (the materialists) said that the material principle is one, and that from this nothing could be caused according to generation and corruption but only according to alteration, it followed that that thing would always remain one according to substance.[1]

Thus, the ancient materialist crudely states all is matter and all changes are quantitative-qualitative alterations of matter. Eduction of material substantial forms is unintelligible to him. He confusedly identifies all causes with matter which escapes him in its identity, and all forms are not substantial but only accidental forms of matter, the one substance. For the modern materialist, of course, there are no such things as substances and causes but only systems of relations in space and time.

The Thomist begins his analysis of the eduction of material substantial forms with the truths known from nature: that finite beings are caused and causes are not in the same genus. He knows that matter cannot be the origin of the eduction of material substantial forms as an agent. Moreover, a mobile being is only an agent when it is operating. Our problem is the permanent source of the material substantial forms and not the transient activity of agents.

The Thomist knows that the material substantial forms do not pre-exist as such; otherwise there would be no problem of the generation of material substantial forms. The seed does not actually exist before its own generation nor does the oxygen educed from water actually exist as a substance before the substance of water is decomposed. Furthermore, the Thomist does not oversimplify the problem by saying that material substantial forms are created and there is no evolution. What can be created is the mobile being and not the material substantial form itself.

What remains as the solution to the problem of the origin of material substantial forms? What else can be said but that material forms are educed from matter as from their subject in

[1] In 1 *Phys.*, lect. 14, n. 2.

whose passive potency they were contained. They are not in matter as in an agent, but they must be in matter in some way. Hence, they are in matter as in passive potency. Passive potency is opposed to active potency. Active potency is in the agent. It is the power to act. Passive potency is in the patient. It is the power to receive the act of the agent.

Reflection upon this principle of the origin of material substantial forms is important to the problems of the evolution of the species. It is important because it tells us that material substantial forms arise through transmutation from potency to act. It is metaphysically certain that no being is moved from potency to act but by a being already in act. For nothing can give what it has not got.

How can a species in a lower order of essence evolve to a species of a higher order of essence, as a non-living species to a living? The passive potency as the point of origin of the alleged new living material substantial form must be acted on by some agent; otherwise how is it to be actualized? Is it energized by its own form? But how can it be changed to a living species since by identity it is of a non-living order. Is it moved by non-living agents or a combination of favorable environmental conditioning factors? But these also are not of the higher order of the living. The materialist answers by simply denying essences. He simplifies the problem by denying the principle of identity at stake. For him, it is all a case of alterations in what he confusedly calls "matter."

There is a certain truth in the materialists assertion, for the only proofs for evolution are in the order of alterations or accidental changes. There is no evidence for the evolution from one inferior species to another higher species: in the order of essence: the non-living to the living, the plant form to the animal, the brute to Man. There are the many "missing links." So long, however, as the meaning of natural species is used confusedly without clear distinction between species in the strict sense as an essence and species in the loose sense as an accidental description within an essence the evolution of the species will remain very nebulous. In a sense this is understandable because the materiality of material substantial forms is an opaque element to human intelligence. This is in part an explanation of the difficulty in the problems of natural species. For example, are all plants made of one essence, or are there distinct essences of plants? To answer this one must be certain as to what essence means in the plant kingdom. Man is still learning.

This much is certain, however, that although modern science abounds in examples of the quantitative-qualitative alterations of mobile beings, there is no evidence of the living being evolved from the passive potency of matter by agents of the non-living order, of man evolving from the lower animals, or of animals evolving from plants. It is a law of the eduction of material substantial forms that they are educed from the passive potency of matter by agents according to the nature of the agents. Natural agents are determined as is the passivity of the second matter of the patient. There is evolution in the cosmos but there is no testimony that it is the evolution of higher essences from the lower, man from the lower mammals, animals from plants, the living from the non-living.

There is nothing repugnant to sound philosophy in the position of Parker and Clarke on the theory of organic evolution in their *Introduction to Animal Biology*:

> This theory as it is now understood holds that plants and animals now in existence are the lineal but modified descendants of plants and animals that existed in bygone ages, and that related forms of today have, through divergent and hereditable modifications, been derived from earlier common ancestors.[1]

IV. DIFFICULTIES CONCERNING THE
EDUCTION OF MATERIAL SUBSTANTIAL FORMS

We noted in the beginning of our tract on hylomorphism that first principles of mobile beings cannot arise from one another. It seems that in the statement of the origin of material substantial forms we are asserting that these substantial forms arise from the material principle. This seems to be a contradiction.

Reply: The contradiction is not real. For we do not assert that material substantial forms arise simply as forms from the material principle but that these forms are produced dependently on matter. Aquinas distinguishes:

> Matter is the cause of the form, insofar as the form exists only in matter. Likewise, the form is the cause of the

---

[1] J. Parker and J. Clarke, *An Introduction to Animal Biology* (2nd edition, St. Louis: C. V. Mosby Company, 1945), pp. 483, 484.

matter, insofar as matter has existence in act only through the form.[2]

In the explanation of the eduction of a material substantial form it is asserted that it is educed from the passivity of matter by the activity of the agent. The active principle of such activity in an agent is an accident as the generative powers of an animal. But an accident cannot educe a substantial form from the potency of matter. Therefore, a substantial form cannot be educed from the passive potency of matter by the activity of an agent.

Reply: The major is distinguished: an active principle of a natural agent is an accidental form which acts as an instrument, we concede; which acts as a principal cause, we deny.

The minor is contradistinguished: an accidental form which acts in virtue of a substantial form as an instrument cannot educe form from the potency of matter, we deny; an accidental form which acts as a principal cause cannot educe a substantial form from the potency of matter, we concede.

Since no creature can operate immediately through its own substance, it follows that in substantial changes the accidental form is the proximate active principle of the natural agent. The proximate principle of a mobile being operates in virtue of the substantial form. An accidental principle as an instrument of the substance is elevated to produce substance. The efficacy of the substantial generation is ascribed to the substantial form. The generative powers, in the living, the chemico-physical qualities in the inorganic—the proximate principles of activity—are instrumental to their substantial form in that they act under the determination of the substantial form. The eduction of a new substance is not essentially the result of qualitative alterations but of substantial change in which a new, material, substantial form is educed out of the passive potency of matter. We shall discuss this process in the following chapter. It suffices here to show that the Thomist is not ascribing substantial changes principally to accidental principles.

V. CONCLUSION

Hylomorphism, therefore, holds that mobile being compounded of prime matter and substantial form is a real substantial unity

[2] St. Thomas Aquinas, *The Principles of Nature*, translated by R. Kocourek, (St. Paul: North Central Publishing Co., 1948), p. 16.

endowed with active and passive powers through which by an inherent tendency it works out its own perfection. Hylomorphism explains the static and dynamic properties of mobile being by the really distinct opposite principles, substantial form and prime matter. These essential parts of mobile being cannot exist separately; they are incomplete principles which complement one another.

Prime matter is not determined in itself; it is pure potentiality and can exist only in the compound along with substantial form. It is not brought into being by change but remains as the subject of new substantial forms. The substantial form actualizes the potentiality of prime matter and is the intrinsic reason why the substance is of one species and not another. Because of it the substance has definite qualities and definite activities. Matter and form thus cause material substance, each in their own way by constituting it. This is effected by the communication of form to matter.

The causality of intrinsic causes is not extrinsic activity, which is exercised by the efficient cause. Once the mobile being is formed in essence, its substantial form can act as an efficient cause. Finally, material substantial forms are educed from the potentiality of matter. Their evolution is constituted by the nature of the agent in act and the passivity of the second matter from which they are drawn.

Suggested Reading

Aristotle: "Physics" Bk. 1, *op. cit,;* "On Generation," Bk. 1, translated by H. Joachim, *op. cit.,* Vol. 2.

St. Thomas Aquinas: *In 1 Phys. op. cit,;* On the Principles of Nature, *op. cit.*

E. Gilson, *The philosophy of St. Thomas Aquinas* (St. Louis: Herder Co., 1939), pp. 186-203.

V. Smith, *Philosophical Physics* (New York: Harper and Brothers, 1950), pp. 139-180.

J. Donceel, "Causality and Evolution" in *The New Scholasticism* XXXIX (1965) 295-315.

Questions

1. State the thesis on hylomorphism.
    a. Define the terms and the meaning of the thesis.
    b. Prove the thesis.
2. Compare the discoveries of experimental science with the hylomorphic thesis of cosmology.
3. Prove that prime matter and substantial form cannot exist separately.
4. What is prime matter considered negatively and positively by Aristotle? Can prime matter be defined adequately? Explain your answer briefly.

5. What are the two kinds of substantial forms? What is meant by the statement that substantial form is the principle of specification, of being and of operation in a mobile being?

6. What do you understand by the origin of material substantial forms? How is this cosmological principle related to the evolution of the species?

7. Answer the following objections:

a. Hylomorphism really distinguishes prime matter from substantial form and then claims that material substantial form proceeds from prime matter.

b. Hylomorphism attributes the origin of the material substantial forms to accidents which by their nature are inferior to material substantial forms.

CHAPTER III

The Substantial Compound

I. Introduction.
II. The Intrinsic Principles of a Substantial Compound in Generation.
　　Thesis 12: The Intrinsic Principles of a Substantial Compound in Generation are Prime Matter, Substantial Form, and Privation.
　　A. Generation and Chemical Change.
　　B. Immediate Union of Matter and Form in the Substantial Compound.
III. The Unity of Form.
　　Thesis 13: Where there is a Substantial Compound there is one Substantial Form; therefore, the Elements cannot be in Act but they Remain Virtually.
　　A. Spectroscopy and the Unicity of the Substantial Form.
　　B. Atomic Theory and the Unicity of the Substantial Form.
　　C. Mass and Energy; Matter and Form.
IV. The Principle of Individuation of the Substantial Compound.
V. Hylosystemism.

I. INTRODUCTION

THE SUBSTANCE of a mobile being is a substantial compound because it has essential parts: prime matter and substantial form. A substantial compound is to be distinguished from a chemico-physical compound which is composed of quantitative parts endowed with various qualities. A chemico-physical compound can be separated into its elementary parts which can exist as wholes. For example, oxygen and hydrogen can exist as distinct entities outside of water. Essential parts, however, always remain incomplete beings; they can never be independently existing beings. As we have already demonstrated, prime matter and substantial form cannot exist by themselves. It is the substantial compound that exists.

Every chemico-physical compound connotes a substantial compound. The distinction between the substantial compound and chemico-physical compound rests in the formalities: the substance in its essential parts is a substantial compound, a substance in its quantitative parts endowed with qualities is viewed as a chemico-physical compound.

II. THE INTRINSIC PRINCIPLES OF A SUBSTANTIAL COMPOUND IN GENERATON

THESIS XII:

The Intrinsic Principles of a Substantial Compound in Generation are Prime Matter, Substantial Form, and Privation.

1. MEANING OF THE THESIS: We assert that the three principles stated in the thesis are required for substantial change. We are formally concerned here with substantial change itself and not with the qualitative changes, which dispose the matter for the substantial change. These latter accidental principles of change are treated in chemistry and physics.

2. EXPLANATION OF TERMS: By "a substantial compound in generation" or in process of coming into being, we mean a mobile being that is substantially changing. The old substantial forms corrupt and the new substantial form is educed, as when water is generated from hydrogen and oxygen. The change is substantial. "Prime matter and substantial form" have been defined. By "privation" is meant the lack of a certain substantial form in a suitable subject. The substantial form of water is lacking to the matter of hydrogen and oxygen in the process of generating water. Privation is called an accidental principle of substantial change or generation. It may be asked, however, how can privation be a real principle since it is a lack of being? But privation is not pure negation of form but the negation of substantial form

in a suitable subject and so it is real. The matter is deprived of a certain form which it is capable of receiving.

Privation ceases when the form is in the subject, that is, when the generation is completed as in the generation of water out of hydrogen and oxygen. Thus the matter of hydrogen and oxygen are capable of receiving the form of water in generation, but they are deprived of this form until their own forms disappear and the new form of water appears.

3. OPPONENTS: All who oppose the hylomorphic thesis, principally the atomists and dynamists.

4. PROOF:

A substantial compound in generation is the substance of a mobile being as it is substantially changing.

But mobile being as substantially changing requires three principles: 1) a common subject, prime matter; 2) a new substantial form to which it naturally tends (the old substantial form corrupts), and 3) privation, the absence of the new form not yet acquired but which is suitable to the matter.

Therefore, prime matter, substantial form and privation are the intrinsic principles of a substantial compound in generation.

Major: Evident from the notion of a mobile being in generation.

Minor: Evident from the principle of sufficient reason. Every substantial change in the universe of mobile beings requires: 1) something common or something that remains throughout the change (otherwise there would be an annihilation of an existing mobile being and the creation of a new mobile being), 2) something substantially new to which it tends while the old substantial form disappears (otherwise it would not be a substantial change), and 3) privation of a new form in a suitable subject (otherwise there would not be given sufficient reason for the appearance of a new form). The new substantial form supplants the old. The corruption of one form is the generation of another, and the generation of one form is the corruption of another. The decomposition of water generates the substances of hydrogen and oxygen.

Substantial change is not simply indeterminate but an ordered process. This presupposes in the subject which passes to a new substantial act a capacity to this rather than to another form, and also supposes in the subject a lack of such a suitable form. For example, the matter of H and O has a capacity to receive the form of water in generation. This form is suitable to such matter. And because the matter of H and O lacks the form of water, we say there is a privation of this form in generation. We do not speak of privation as a principle of the *constitution* of mobile beings but rather as a principle in their *generation* because the generation is not completed or has not achieved the substantial term to which it is tending.

A. GENERATION AND CHEMICAL CHANGE. When the chemist studies the generation of substances, he does so through an analysis of their qualitative-quantitative changes. The frontiers of his analysis are described by certain chemico-physical alterations in mobile beings which may indicate new substances. The chemist has the same subject as the cosmologist but his method and object are distinct.

No new substance arises if a few drops of mercury and a little sulphur are gently stirred in a mortar. The result is an accidental union or a mixture. The particles of sulphur can be readily distinguished from the mercury and it can be safely inferred that no generation of a new substance has occurred. But take a pestle and vigorously grind the two substances together and a decided change takes place. The substance formed is black. Mercury and sulphur no longer can be distinguished as distinct substances. In this experiment there is evidenced a definite change from the notably proper accidental forms of sulphur and mercury to the notably proper accidental forms of mercuric sulphide.

There is no immediate evidence of change from one substantial form to another, for substances do not operate immediately. Chemical analysis reports the changes in properties. Certain accidents as instruments of the substantial forms of mercury and sulphur have acted and the corruption of these elements *instantaneously* gave rise to the generation of the new form of mercuric sulphide. In such cases, the successive changes reported in the laboratory are the accidental changes principally of quantity and quality which precede, accompany and succeed substantial changes.

The fact that generation is not a haphazard process but an ordered process is evidenced in experiments. Sulphur and mercury combine in a definite proportion. That the proportion used by nature in making this compound is definite or fixed may be proved by adding more mercury and continuing the grinding. When there is an excess of mercury the particles which will not combine are easily seen. It is evident that the proportion of the elements in a compound is fixed. Proximately this is accounted for by the qualities or powers of mobile beings. Ultimately it is explained by the first principle of operation, by the substantial form. There is a definite proximate aptitude for the reception of the new form in the matter of mercury and sulphur.

Chemistry offers a descriptive picture of such alterations or changes in properties which connote generation of substances. Equations, which symbolically express these changes, indicate generation. For example, the fact that mercury combines with sulphur may be expressed as follows: $Hg+S=HgS$. It must be noted, however, that the chemist has no direct report of generation because substances do not operate immediately. Those chemists who are dynamists in their view of nature deny substantial change. They argue that they observe only changes in weight, color, taste and other qualitative and quantitative characteristics as if substantial change must be on the same level as these accidental changes in order to be real, an evident impossibility. Actually, substantial changes are inferred; they are not observed.

The dynamist's thinking crudely assumes that the only technique for reaching truth is the direct reports of the empirico-metric method, and that the experimental sciences can tell us everything about the universe that can be told. But the universe of mobile being is deeper in its reality than the material accidents, for these are avenues to the very core of mobile being. A man cannot travel along these avenues to the basic comprehension of substantial change without the special equipment of cosmology.

B. THE IMMEDIATE UNION OF MATTER AND FORM IN THE SUBSTANTIAL COMPOUND. Existence and essence of a mobile being are immediately united. Can the same be said concerning the union of prime matter and substantial form or is there an intermediary principle that unites them? It must be noted that here we are dealing with essential union or formal union and not effective union or union that is the effect of an agent; for it is certain that matter and form are mediately united by the action of an agent.

PROOF:

> Matter is essentially potency and form is essentially act.
> But potency and act are immediately united.
> Therefore, matter and form are immediately united.

Major: Evident from the definitions of matter and form.

Minor: The essence of matter precisely is to receive the form; as we have seen, it is pure potency and the essence of form is precisely to determine or actuate the matter. There is no reason for an intermediary principle. We cannot multiply principles without necessity. There would be no sufficient reason for another principle since the matter as the principle of reception receives and the form as the principle of determination acts or determines the matter.

III. THE UNITY OF FORM

There is an age old great dispute among the Scholastics concerning the plurality of substantial forms in a substantial compound. Does a mobile being have one substantial form or many? Is there a superior substantial form in a compound along with inferior substantial forms? Can a mobile being be at the same time specifically one and many?

THESIS XIII:

Where there is a Substantial Compound there is One Substantial form; therefore, the Elements cannot be in Act but they Remain Virtually.

1. MEANING OF THE THESIS: In this thesis we are not considering whether elements are substances, nor are we arguing the problem: Do substantial compounds exist? Our problem here is simply whether or not each substantial compound has one substantial form.

2. EXPLANATION OF TERMS: "Substantial compound" is that which arises from other substances and formally constitutes a specific and individual essence. Water is a substantial compound which

arises out of the substances of hydrogen and oxygen. It is really opposed to a mixture, an accidental union in which the substances remain, as in a mixture of sugar and water.

"One substantial form" means that it is formally and actually one, a unique form in number and species.

"Element" can be understood in the absolute sense: a mobile being into which all mobile beings can be resolved and which cannot be resolved physically into a simpler form. In this thesis, however, we use the term in the relative sense, that is, for mobile beings into which compounds can be dissolved, the elements of the periodic table of Mendeleef. When we say the elements cannot be in act, we mean they cannot actually conserve their substantial forms in a substantial compound.

"The elements remain virtually" the elements are not in merely remote potency in a substantial compound; they exist in proximate potency as qualities of the compound in such a way that the compound can be reduced back into these elements from which it has arisen. Oxygen is in water not as a substance but in the proximate potency of the substance, water.

3. OPPONENTS: Avicebron (1020-1070), a Jewish philosopher of renown, taught the plurality of substantial forms in a compound. The Oxford Scholastics, notably Robert Grosseteste, Chancellor of Oxford, (1175-1253) and the Franciscans, Thomas of York (-1260), Roger Bacon (1214-1294), John Peckham (-1292) were also opponents of the unicity of substantial form in the compound. They taught various kinds of pluralism. Duns Scotus (1265/66-1308) held that besides the rational soul which is the substantial form, there is the substantial form of the body disposing the body for the higher form, the soul.[1]

Dynamists who deny substantial unity completely are not direct adversaries of this thesis because they do not admit substantial forms at all.

4. PROOF: *Part* 1:

From the notion of substantial form and of substantial compound:

Where there is a substantial compound there is one essence. But where there is one essence, there is one substantial form.

---

[1] *Opus Oxoniense,* 4, 11, 3, nos. 54 ff.

Therefore, where there is a substantial compound there is one substantial form.

Major: Evident from the notion of substantial compound. In a substantial compound only one essence exists. If there were more than one essence it would be an aggregate or accidental union of substances. Accidental union of substances such as a union of oil and water are mixtures rather than substantial compounds.

Minor: Where there is one essence there is one specifying principle or one act giving specific substantial being. Where there is one specific substantial act there is one substantial form, for form is the first act of matter, or it gives matter its substantial specification to be what it is and not something else.

Let us suppose there were many substantial forms in a substantial compound, then each would constitute a thing in different determined grades of being. Hence, one thing at the same time would be actually many things substantially; it would be formally in diverse grades of being at the same time like the mythical faun.

PROOF: *Part 2*:

If a compound is substantial, its elements either do not remain at all or they remain actually and formally or they remain only in remote potency or they remain virtually (i.e. in proximate potency).

But neither the first nor the second nor the third can be, but only the fourth.

Therefore, the elements in a substantial compound remain virtually.

Major: Evident from the fact that all metaphysical possibilities are cited.

Minor: Elements in some way remain in the substantial compound as experimental science shows by analysis—hydrogen and oxygen are in some way in water. Elements do not remain actually as substances in a substantial compound. We demonstrated in the first part of the proof that in a substantial compound there is only one substantial form. Nor do elements remain in a substantial compound in remote potency but they are there virtually. For if elements remain in a compound according to mere potency, or indifference, then the term of the corruptive act or dissolution of a substantial compound would not be diverse according to the nature of the compound but according to the diversity of agents. On the contrary, the compound always dissolves in some way into elements from which it was generated. H_2O corrupts into H and O and it does not dissolve into these elements formally because of the agents that act upon it, but because of the nature of the compound H_2O itself. Hence, it remains that H and O exist in the substantial compound of water virtually or qualitatively. Active and passive dispositions are in H_2O which place this compound in proximate potency to resolution into its elements.

The doctrine of the unicity of substantial form is confirmed by the teaching of St. Thomas Aquinas:

> It is manifest, moreover, that a thing has being through form and through form it has unity, and on account of this reason, wherever there is a multitude of forms, there is not one being simply . . .[1]

A. SPECTROSCOPY AND THE UNICITY OF THE SUBSTANTIAL FORM. Spectroscopy is a branch of physical science which investigates spectra. Spectra may be regarded as the product of the resolution of the composite luminous radiations into more homogeneous components. Any one physical substance always produces a line or lines of the same color; in fact, a line in exactly the same part of the spectrum. No two elements have identical systems of stripes in their characteristic spectra just as no two persons have identical finger prints. In the case of the elements in a compound, each gives its own spectra undisturbed by the presence of others, except that the spectra of the most abundant element is usually strongest and those elements which are present in very small amounts may furnish only their strongest lines and these faintly. The lines of each element occur in groups with a recognizable pattern in regard to position and relative intensity.

There are Scholastics who argue that the presence of the spectra of the elements in a compound is proof that the elements remain formally in the compound. In reply, we concede that it is a scientific fact that the spectra of the elements endure in some way. But the presence of such spectra is not adequate ground for arguing to the presence of the substantial forms of the elements in a compound. The substantial form of the com-

---

[1] Quodl. I, q. 4, a.6.c.

pound retains the elements virtually and their characteristics show up in the qualitative analysis of the compound's spectra. These qualities manifest in their line spectra a definite strength or faintness due to the proper qualities that specify the compound. Spectra of elements in compounds and of the elements by themselves are not identical. The difference is not casual or incidental. The principle of specification in the compound formally causes the difference. The substantial form specifies the qualities of spectra proper to a compound with a recognizable pattern in regard to position and relative intensity.

The assertion that the spectra of elements noted in a compound imply that a compound has as many substantial forms as there are spectra of elements, neglects the full picture of their specification. This specification cannot be explained on the substantial level by substantial forms because these would specify independent patterns of activity, but there is a specific unity of the pattern of spectra of a compound which results from the substantial unity of the compound.

The Bohr model of hydrogen shows that the electron directly is much more determinative of the emission of the various spectral lines than the nucleus of the atom. However, the whole atom of hydrogen is somehow at work in determining the lines which this atom emits. The same electron in another atom would not act the same way under the same excitation. The specific character of the emissions of the spectral lines is taken from the atom in its specific unity.

B. ATOMIC THEORY AND THE UNICITY OF THE SUBSTANTIAL FORM. Atoms in isolation or in the free state act as independent mobile beings. Their sub-atomic particles (electrons, protons, neutrons and the other known particles) are integral parts of the atom's substantial being. These particles are virtually present in the atom, that is they are qualities or dynamic accidents of the atomic substance. They are not substances heaped together in the atom.

The molecule manifests a unicity which demonstrates that it is not simply a heap of particles. If we consider a molecule of hydrogen constituted from two atoms, we find that its specific heat is 4.8 calories. Since the specific heat of each atom is 3 calories, then the specific heat of a molecule of H should be 6 calories if a molecule of H is only an aggregate, an accidental union of atoms. The specific properties of the molecule of H argues for a specific being with its own substantial form.

The mode of action of the atoms outside the molecule is different from their mode of acting as integral parts of the molecule. In a molecule, as in the case of H with two atoms, the atoms act as parts of a system. Molecules are not merely sums or haphazard heaps of atoms.

The atoms of the various elements exhibit a definite heterogeneity all the way from hydrogen to nobelium. Hydrogen emits its peculiar spectra in which its electron has more to do than the atomic nucleus. But the same electron in another atom would act differently under the same excitation. The unity of the atom manifests its unique substantial being through its proper activities. The atom is not a mere heap of particles which have casually come together. It is not an accidental aggregate but a substantial whole.

The principles of the sub-atomic particles when they are considered in themselves manifest poorer properties than those which are evidenced in the atom itself. On the scale of mobile being the atom is superior to the sub-atomic particles as indeed the compound is superior to the elements. As Aquinas remarks in his opusculum *On the Hidden Works of Nature*: "... and thus in a constant ascension, the nobler the specific form, the more excellent the powers and operations proceeding from it...."

When an atom is outside a molecule and when an electron is found outside an atom, then the atom and the electron can be considered as individual substances. They show themselves to be independent of any formal unity except their own. (Note the experiments of Aston concerning protons and Millikan concerning electrons.) When the electrons are in the atom, certain orbits are possible for them, and their energy varies by leaps; outside the atom all orbits are possible and their energy can vary continuously.

The atom in the free state is not merely an aggregate of electrons moving around a nucleus but truly an individual substance, a continuous being although composed of heterogeneous parts. Its particles or integral parts are united in a "field," the electrical or the magnetic field. These particles are not separate substances heaped in an aggregate with really empty spaces between them.

Care must be taken not to interpret the models of the atom constructed by the physicist as if they were real reports of the physical worlds. There is some correspondence to reality. The model is serviceable insofar as it projects what the physicist is attempting to convey. The picture of the integral parts of the atom such as the following diagram of helium is not a photograph, so to speak, of the atom:

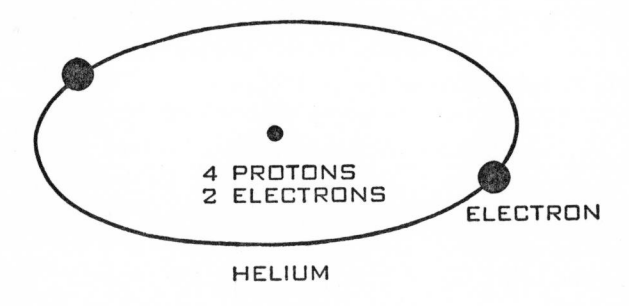

4 PROTONS
2 ELECTRONS
ELECTRON

HELIUM

This is a logical-real schema built up with some foundation in the real. It reports the atom according to a certain abstract pattern which in some way corresponds to it although not strictly. This, of course, is to be expected of such a schema because our knowledge of the sub-atomic world is still in its initial stages. The comparison of this schema to the universe is imaginative to say the least. There is some connection, but it is slight; the universe is not a substance as is the atom.

The Bohr theory of the atom describes how an electron in an outer orbit of the atom can be excited into a more remote orbit by suitable means. When it falls back to its former orbit it does not do so continuously but by a leap, and a quantum of light is emitted in the process. This is noteworthy because the quantum is not protruded little by little but all at once and so the electron is thought to move discontinuously. However, is this apparent discontinuity real or is it conceptual? Is it due to the hazy character of the Bohr theory which postulates discontinuous movement of the electron because a clear knowledge of this motion is lacking? The obscurity of the Bohr theory favors the latter interpretation rather than the bold assertion that the Bohr picture describes reality in this case.

There always will be difficulties in the illustration of the hylomorphic doctrine as new fields of study are opened up in experimental science. The Thomist cannot clear away these difficulties by the art of his method. They are in part inherent in the obscurity of new theories in the experimental field and also somewhat due to the limitations of our insight into the material substantial forms. On the other hand, these difficulties should not be exaggerated to the plane of real doubts of proved objections against hylomorphism. Hylomorphism by its very nature is not an experimental thesis. Furthermore, as a philosophical thesis, it does not claim to give complete comprehension of the essence of the mobile. Hylomorphism as a philosophical thesis is demonstrable so far as it goes.

There have been Scholastics who would "prove" hylomorphism by experimental science as those who held that the nucleus and electron-periphrey of hydrogen, for example, are as matter and form respectively of the substance. But the nucleus and electron-periphery are integral-qualitative and not essential parts of the substance of hydrogen. They are secondary and not primary. There are Scholastics who, when they hear the experimentalist speak of a strange binding force that retains the atomic parts in a unity, offer the solution that it is all a case in proof of the substantial form. Ultimately, in the constitution of the atom the substantial form explains the specification of its essential unity. But the experimentalist will never discover this by his methods. In time one can safely predict that he will discover proximate principles, which will satisfy his limited quest for the binding force in the atom. Substantial form will never be revealed to the experimentalist as such.

Although truth is the object of all science, there are certain kinds of truth open to a science according to its object. The experimentalist is not destined to discover substantial forms nor will the philosopher find proofs for substantial form in experimental reports. Confirmations of hylomorphism, however, can be found in the experimental sciences.

C. MASS AND ENERGY; MATTER AND FORM. $E = MC^2$ is sometimes invoked as a proof that what we call mobile being is simply energy. This formula was developed by Einstein from his theory that mass varies with motion. E represents energy; M, mass; and C, the velocity of light. Accordingly one pound of uranium if transformed into energy and properly harnessed would yield enough to meet the total electrical needs of the United States for several weeks. It was experimentation along these lines that led to the atomic bomb.

Now the equation $E=MC^2$ is not meant to report on what mobile being is in itself. Actually, this equation deals with qualitative-quantitative changes in mobile being and not the conversion of matter into simple energy. Mass does not mean matter but rather a quantum which is measured by energy. A quantum is not a material substance as we have demonstrated in the first thesis.

Energy and mass are phases of mobile being. "The Conservation of Energy" law states that energy can be changed but not destroyed. "The Conservation of Matter" law states that matter can be altered in form but not destroyed. "Matter" in this context really means mass or the amount of a mobile being that is measured. These two laws now become one law, which simply states that mass and energy are forms of the same thing and that change is possible between these forms as well as within them, though mass-energy could not be destroyed. The thing of which these two forms are predicated is the essentially static-dynamic dualism: the hylomorphic substance of mobile being.

Interesting to note is the existence of a nuclear field energy quantum which would appear as a particle with a mass of 300 to 400 x the mass of the electron and which was predicted by the distinguished Japanese physicist, Hideki Yukawa. The mass 313 meson fills Yukawa's prediction. This will no doubt seem strange as a weighable particle. As our knowledge of the sub-atomic world increases, we come to understand more and more how it does not fit into the over-simplified picture of "the simple energy theory" as described by the dynamists. Mechanism confused quanta and substance; dynamism confuses energy and the mobile.

IV. THE PRINCIPLE OF INDIVIDUATION OF

THE SUBSTANTIAL COMPOUND

Although considered in metaphysics, the individuation of the substantial compound also merits the attention of the cosmologist.

Our problem concerns what makes this mobile being to be this mobile being and not another? From the most minute sub-atomic particle to the heavenly body of the greatest magnitude there is individuation of mobile being. What is the ultimate principle of individuation in beings compounded in their essence from matter and form.

It should be noted that we are seeking the ultimate reason of individuation. It would not do, therefore, merely to affirm that this mobile being is this mobile being because of its particular position, weight, figure and so forth. We are not seeking the externals of individuality but the ultimate principle of it.

In the opusculum, *On Being and Essence*, St. Thomas says that matter is the principle of individuation but not prime matter as such.[1] Rather it is what the Angelic Doctor calls "signate matter" or matter with its parts outside of parts (extension), with its order of parts (*situs*), and considered under dimensions. This doctrine is commonly taught by the Thomists. There is a difference of opinion, however, as to what is meant by signate matter under its dimensions. The commentator on the *Contra Gentiles*, Ferrara, taught that it is matter actuated and existing under its actual dimensions.[2] On the other hand, Cajetan and John of St. Thomas assert that the matter concerned is only in potency to this quantity rather than to that but is is not yet actuated.[3]

It would seem that the opinion of Cajetan and John of St. Thomas is untenable because it seems to be the same as to say that prime matter individuates form. It is not clear why prime matter should have a definite order to this rather than to that quantity.

The solution seems to be the opinion of Ferrara. The great commentator on the *Contra Gentiles* does not say that matter exists without form when he affirms that matter exists first and individuates the form. He is concerned here with a mode of intrinsic causality. Causality in this order is mutual and simultaneous. The form gives the specific perfection and the "to be," and the matter at the same time limits and individuates. However, we should not attempt to imagine first of all something

---

[1] *On Being and Essence,* ch. 2.
[2] In 1 *Contra Gentiles,* ch. 21.
[3] In 1 *Summa Theologica,* q. 29, a.l. *Cursus Philosophicus,* Philosophia Naturae, P. 2, q. 9, nos. 3, 4.

we call signate matter as an existing entity to which we add form which is thereby individuated. It must be realized that the principle of individuation cannot be imagined; rather it is conceived. Imagination is limited to the sensible. Intrinsic principles of mobile being precede the sensible in nature. The real sequence here is abstracted by the mind.

Matter in act and extended by reason of its quantity under dimensions (as a condition) is individual matter. St. Thomas explains what he means by the dimensions of quantity that bring about this matter rather than that in the following passage of his *Commentary on the Trinity*.

> ... matter is made this and signate in so far as it has dimensions. Now these dimensions can be considered in two ways. On the one hand, they can be considered according to a definite size and shape: and thus, as perfect beings, they are placed in the genus of quantity: thus they cannot be the principle of individuation, because such a termination varies in the individual and it would follow that the individual does not always remain exactly the same. On the other hand, the dimensions can be considered interminate only in the nature of dimension, although they can never be without termination ... and thus they are placed in the genus of quantity but only as imperfect. From these interminate dimensions is brought about this matter, signate matter, and thus it individuates the form.[1]

The principle of individuation, therefore, is found ultimately in the matter rather than in the form; in the matter that is quantified rather than in prime matter considered by itself and in matter that is quantified under interminate dimensions rather than in terminate dimensions. One cannot identify individuation on a time scale as one can identify the actualization of some mode of efficient causality of the mobile. We are dealing with a type of principle that is intrinsic and which is conceived on the scale of the order of nature rather than on the time-scale of activity.

For example, this man is this man not because of his substantial form, but rather because of the material principle that is in him, which limits and individuates. But it cannot be the prime matter of this man simply that individuates him in that prime matter is itself indifferent. Why should pure potency

[1] In *De Trin.* q. 4, a. 2.

have an order to this rather than to that quantity? It is in the quantified matter that we must look for the principle of individuation, the matter that is in act and that is divided from others, while it is actually undivided in itself. But it cannot be terminated matter under this particular set of dimensions for the reason that such matter varies while the individual man does not vary as an individual, which would have to be the case if terminated matter would be the principle of individuation. This man, Peter, does not become another individual by changes of height, weight, and so forth. Thus the principle of individuation of this man must be found in matter under quantity of interminate dimensions which is conceived although not sensibly perceived; for what is perceived is already the individual sensible mobile being.

V. HYLOSYSTEMISM

There are modern cosmologists such as A. Mitterer of Munich, who believe that hylomorphism is inadequate to explain the ultimate constitution of inorganic substances. And so these men have substituted a theory called hyloststemism in its place. Hylomorphism considers a mobile being as a composite substance consisting of prime matter and substantial form. Hylosystemism views it as an atomary-energy system working as a functional unit. But what is meant by an atomary-energy system? The new physics does not regard the atom as ultimate. How can a cosmologist speak of it as a primary principle in the intrinsic constitution of mobile being itself?

These critics assert that hylomorphism consists in a dualistic conception of mobile being; hyloststemism has a pluralistic conception. The hylosystemist asserts that his pluralism is more in accord with the findings of modern physics. In response to this the defender of hylomorphism can reply: it is true that hylomorphism is dualistic in respect to the intrinsic principles of the essential composition of mobile being itself but this is not in contradiction to the plurality of integral parts with diverse qualities found in mobile being in its accidental characteristics by the experimental sciences. Essential composition and accidental composition do not mean the same thing.

Hylomorphism, it is charged, brings about complete homogeneity in the substance; hylosystemism accounts for a heterogeneity of parts in varying degrees of coordination and sub-ordination. But it must be answered to this criticism that hy-lomorphism does not deny heterogeneity. St. Thomas observes that a thing can be "one in subject and many according to its accidents."[1] There is no repugnance to be found in the statement there is one substantial form in a mobile being but many different accidental forms. Substantial form and accidental form are not one and the same thing.

The statement of the hylosystemist that the hylomeric body is a system of corporeal substances shows that hylosystemism is not really explaining the constitution of mobile being but assert-ing that larger bodies are constituted from smaller bodies. But our problem is the essence of mobile being rather than a de-lineation of the great and the small in the genus of the mobile.

Hylosystemism explains generation in terms of radioactive elements that change spontaneously with no outside force in-fluencing the change. The Thomist does not deny that radio-active elements have a definite role to play in alteration and generation. But the Thomist does not explain generation simply in terms of these. He goes beyond the powers of mobile beings to substantial principles of prime matter and substantial form. We have already discussed this in our treatment of the in-strumental causes acting under the influence of the substantial form in generation.

The complex data given by the experimental sciences on mobile being do not contradict the hylomorphic doctrine. The plurality in the accidental order does not negate the duality of matter and form in the substantial order. There must not be a confusion of these two orders. If we are to substitute hylosystem-ism for hylomorphism because of the pluralism of an atomary-energy system, we are failing to distinguish properly between substance and accidents and we are substituting the method of physics for the method of cosmology. It is all a case of the fallacy of the uniform method. Hylosystemism is really a form of dyna-mism under a new label which has become somewhat popular largely through its use of modern scientific terms; unfortunately these terms have been lifted far out of context.

Suggested Reading

St. Thomas Aquinas, *On the Principles of Nature*, (translated by

[1] *S. Theol.* P. 1, q. 11, a. 2.

R. Kocourek) *op. cit., Summa Theologica*, P. 1, q. 118, a. 2, ad 2; P. 1, q. 85, a. 4.

D. Sharp, *Franciscan Philosophy at Oxford* (London: Oxford University Press, 1930).

C. Bittle. *From Aether to Cosmos* (Milwaukee: The Bruce Publishing Company, 1941), pp. 315-342.

F. Renoirte. *Cosmology. Translated* by J. Coffey (New York: J. Wagner, Inc., 1950), pp. 3-37.

J. I. Shannon, S.J., *The Amazing Electron* (Milwaukee, Bruce, 1946).

Questions

1. Distinguish the substantial compound studied by the cosmologist from a qualitative-quantitative compound studied by the experimentalist.
2. State the thesis on the unicity of the substantial form.
    a. What is the meaning of the thesis?
    b. Explain the terms.
    c. Who are the opponents?
    d. Prove the thesis in its two parts.
3. How do you reconcile the fact that spectroscopy shows the spectra of the elements in a substantial compound, if only one substantial form exists in the substantial compound?
4. How can the atom be considered a unity and yet a plurality in its particles? Delineate this unity briefly as an illustration of substantial unity. Can it be objectively maintained that vacua exist in the atom's structure?
5. Cite some contemporary attempts to prove hylomorphism from the data of the new physics. Evaluate these attempts.
6. Discuss the mass-energy duality and the doctrine of matter and form.
7. What individuates a mobile being? Explain and illustrate your answer.
8. Evaluate hylosystemism as a philosophical theory of the nature of the mobile.

Part Two

The Extrinsic Principles of the Universe of Mobile Being

Section 1

The Efficient Cause of the Universe of Mobile Being: God the Creator

AFTER THE tract on the ultimate intrinsic principles of mobile being, it remains for cosmology to treat of the extrinsic principles of this kind of being. We come now to the problems of the efficient and final causes of the cosmos. In the preceding part we have given an answer to the question: what is the essence of mobile being? But this problem of essence does not exhaust the attention of the cosmologist. The comprehension of mobile being as an entity composed of prime matter and substantial form does not answer the problem of its origin and destiny. Hylomorphism informs us of the matter-form dualism in explaining what a mobile being is, but it is insufficient in explaining the cause by which such an essence exists and the cause on account of which it exists.

In this section we are concerned with the problem of the first efficient cause of the mobile. In Chapter One we shall consider false systems which have endeavored to regard the cosmos as self-sufficient. These systems are generally classed as pantheistic and materialistic. They sometimes disguise themselves under the name of agnosticism. We shall rationally reject these systems. In Chapter Two we shall demonstrate creationism, which alone answers the problem of the ultimate origin of things.

Care must be taken to distinguish the problem of the origin of all mobile being from that of cosmogony or the problem of the origin of the earth, our galaxy, or the order of the heavens in their present state. Our problem concerns the origin of all being in sensible matter and motion rather than some mode of mobile being.

Pseudo-Cosmologies of a Self-Sufficient Universe

I. PANTHEISM

THESIS XIV:

Pantheism Must be Rejected.

1. MEANING OF THE THESIS: Pantheism is against reason and experience, and on these grounds we assert that it is to be rejected.

2. EXPLANATION OF TERMS: Pantheism holds that the universe is God either entirely or partly or as the ideal state to which the world is evolving. In its contemporary meaning, it often speaks of God as evolving in the world, a finite God. Pantheism is of various kinds and may be divided into the following classes:

a) Real Pantheism which includes: Immanent emanationism, as evidenced in the philosophy of Spinoza, which holds that the world is an emanation of the divine reality. God successively produces in Himself various modes and affections. The world, however, is something real.

Transient emanationism, as in neo-platonism, which maintains that the world, which is real, emanates from God as rays from the sun; it is distinct from God and divine. The Hylozoism of the Stoics which asserts that God is the soul of the world is also an example of transient emanationism.

b) Evolutionary Pantheism, the doctrine that God does not yet exist. He is the ideal state to which the world is tending.

Professor Alexander of Manchester in the Gifford Lectures of 1916-18 expressed this view.

c) Ideal Pantheism such as Brahmanism of India—whatever exists is Brahma, and what is not Brahma is only illusion.

d) Transcendental Pantheism which teaches that the unique reality is the knowing subject. Johann Fichte speaks of the world as the mere phenomena of the Ego. For Friedrich Schelling, the unique existent is "absolute identity" which is at the same time real and ideal. For Georg Hegel the unique existing subject is "logical idea" or the notion of being, and by the process of dialectic this notion evolves into all determinate beings (Panlogism.)

3. OPPONENTS: Those who profess Christian Science, Theosophy, and the various philosophical systems cited above. To these we may add absolute dynamists and materialists who believe that the cosmos is self-sufficient.

4. PROOF:

The mobile cosmos can never be identified with Immobile Being, Pure Act, God.

But Pantheism identifies the mobile cosmos with Immobile Being, Pure Act, God.

Therefore, Pantheism is to be rejected.

Major: Evident from theodicy. The cosmos of mobile beings considered in itself is not the Immobile Being, the necessary Divine Being—rather its mobility depends upon the latter. God is called immobile not because of the immobility of inertia but because He is supreme actuality or perfection. The mobile can never be self-sufficient or ultimate in that mobility connotes potency and act, as we have seen. The mobile lacks sufficient reason for its being exactly because it contains potency; it is not purely act, perfection, reality. Hence, the mobile is imperfect, insufficient, and cannot be identified with the perfect, the self-sufficient, the Immobile Being, Pure Act. The infinite multiplication of the mobile does not change its nature of insufficiency precisely because it is mobile.

Minor: Evident from the exposition of pantheism, which either totally or partially identifies the cosmos and God, Who is the

Immobile Being, Pure Act. Pantheism does not adequately define God and the cosmos. It fails to comprehend God as Pure Act because it fails to understand actuality itself. It fails to comprehend the mobile cosmos in terms of the dualism of potency and act because of its monistic tendency to view the cosmos either as purely fieristic, undetermined, potential, or as purely static, and determined.

Pantheism takes being as univocal. As M. Maeterlinck's "Bluebird of Paradise" says of the cosmos: "It is all the same somehow." But the Pantheist never defines objectively what is meant by "the same somehow." The Thomist objectively notes that being is analogous. God's existence, which is identical with His essence, does not exhaust all the possibilities of existence since there exist natures which possess existence, not in their own right as natures, but by participation in existence from God Who is existence itself. It is true that whatever is real is one, but this unity is analogous. God is one in the purest ontological unity. The cosmos is one accidentally as a union of many substances. Man is one in species, but many in individuals. This man is one as a person, but many in the potential parts that compose him physically.

II. MATERIALISM

THESIS XV:

Materialism Must be Rejected

1. MEANING OF THE THESIS: The thesis asserts that materialism is repugnant to reason.

2. EXPLANATION OF TERMS: Materialism holds that everything is one kind of being, namely matter, and that matter is eternal and unproduced. The term "materialist" was first used by Robert Boyle in his work on *The Excellence and Grounds of the Mechanical Philosophy,* 1674.

The atomism of Leucippus and Democritus is the first known formulation of the materialistic philosophy. These ancient Greeks were the first to maintain in a philosophical system that the totality of reality is purely material. It was in France in the eighteenth century that the great modern development of philosophical materialism took place in the writings of Lamettrie and the Encyclopedists. Baron d'Holbach's *Systeme de la Nature*, published in 1770, represents the culmination of the movement. After the accession of the Idealists in Germany at the beginning of the nineteenth century, materialism began to arise again; about the middle of the century Herbert Vogt and Freidrich Buchner were among the leaders. The English agnostics and evolutionists, Herbert Spencer, John Tyndall and Thomas Huxley, can hardly be classed as anything but materialists. In our time Marxian communism is the great exponent of the materialist trend in what is called dialectical materialism. This theory maintains that matter has existed eternally and is a unity of opposites, a composite of contradictory elements. Atheistic communism holds that matter is by its nature autodynamic; there is no need for a Creator.

3. OPPONENTS: All who profess materialistic philosophy in any form as cited above.

4. PROOF:

The corporeal universe is mutable, contingent, finite and composed of many beings.

But such a universe is not the ultimate sufficient cause of itself.

Therefore, materialism which asserts that the corporeal universe is ultimately self-sufficient, must be rejected.

Major: Evident from the first part of cosmology where we have shown that the corporeal universe is accidentally and substantially mutable, that the universe is not infinite, and that it is composed of mobile beings which are specifically and numerically many.

Minor: A mutable, finite, contingent being or a series of such beings is not independent because it is not purely actual. Hence, it is by another (*ens ab alio*). In other words, it is not the ultimate sufficient cause of itself.

Materialism is a species of pantheism. There is no real difference between the propositions; "All is God" and "there is no God but only matter exists." Extremes meet. The materialist denies a personal God, really distinct from the universe. For him matter is autodynamic, self-sufficient and therefore divine. He ascribes to matter the divine attributes of a Necessary Being. Out of this pseudo-cosmology he constructs a false religion of naturalism in which his highest concept is "mother nature."

III. AGNOSTICISM

Agnosticism is the "one floor" view of reality, the belief that physical science alone represents the field of the knowable and religion represents the unknowable. Thomas Huxley who invented the term "agnosticism" explains its meaning in the following words:

> ...It is wrong for a man to say that he is certain of the objective truth of any proposition unless he can produce evidence which logically justifies that certainty. This is what Agnosticism asserts, and in my opinion it is all that is essential to Agnosticism.[1]

Let us distinguish this verbal affirmation of agnosticism from its historical significance. The agnostics, Huxley in England and Haeckel in Germany, were in fact materialists. Their agnosticism is simply a polite name for materialism.

The agnostic claims to be indifferent to God as the Deist claimed that God is indifferent to man. But the human mind cannot be indifferent to the ultimate origin and end of things. Man cannot dismiss these questions as simply "unknown values" that will take thousands of years to answer, if they are ever to be answered. He will identify the Alpha and Omega of all things with matter or some other thing if he turns from belief in a personal God.

It is somewhat a fad in our times for a scientist who espouses materialism to cloak his identity before the public at least by labelling himself an agnostic. This ruse has been indulged in by many who have proven themselves experts in some field of natural science but have unhappily wandered off into a form of evolutionary materialism. Such men condemn creationism and revealed religion in their writings not from the standpoint of explicit atheism but from the rather coy scepticism that "as scientists" they have never found proofs for such doctrines and consequently they have no belief in them. This

---

[1] Thomas Huxley, *Essays Upon Controverted Questions* (New York: D. Appleton & Co., 1892), p. 450.

pseudo-scientific authoritarianism can only be answered by inducing these agnostics to affirm their real position as professed atheists and to answer them accordingly.

Suggested Reading

Aristotle, "Metaphysics," Bk. 12, ch. 6, *op. cit.*

St. Thomas Aquinas: *Summa Theologica*, P. 1, q. 3. a. 8. *Contra Gentiles*, Bk. 1, ch. 21.

Fulton Sheen: *Religion Without God* (New York: Longmans, Green and Co., 1928), p. 3 and ff.

Henri De Lubac, *The Drama of Atheistic Humanism*, translated by E. Riley (London: Sheed and Ward, 1949), pp. 79-127.

Klubertanz and Holloway, *Being and God* (N. Y. Appleton-Century-Crofts, 1963), pp. 362-368.

Questions

1. Define the problem of the efficient cause of the cosmos.
2. Define Pantheism and summarize its principle schools of thought.
3. Prove that Pantheism in any form is false.
4. Define materialism and cite some representative materialists in the history of philosophy.
5. Prove that materialism in any form must be rejected.
6. What is meant by agnosticism? Analyze the agnostic's position.

CHAPTER II

Creationism

I. The Creation of the Universe.
    Thesis 16: The Corporeal Universe was
        Created by God.
II. Problems Related to Creation.
    A. Creation and Time.
    B. Creation and the Eternity of the World.
    C. Entropy.
    D. Creation and Evolution.
    E. The Anti-Proton and "the Annihilation
        of Matter."

I. THE CREATION OF THE UNIVERSE

THERE IS PROBABLY no more profound truth in the natural order than that of creation. In its proper meaning it signifies that everything that exists outside of God, of His own free Will He created out of nothing for His glory and purely of His goodness. Whereas the sculptor makes a statue, he does not make it out of nothing. He takes the marble, which he did not make, and gives it a certain determination. The sculptor does not create the statue, he does not produce its total being. The sculptor is not a creator; he is a wonderful transformer. The engineer, who constructs an edifice, does not create it. He brings together in a certain order the materials which he did not produce. Parents do not create their child; they generate their offspring. The matter of the child was pre-existent.

In creation something is drawn from nothing. Although conceivable, this truth was not conceived by the pagan philosophers. Like many other basic philosophical truths it became known to the human mind through God's revelation to man and then rationally understood in the study of the cosmos. Here we witness the historical relation of faith and reason which is so grossly misunderstood by many contemporary thinkers. These thinkers have become so authoritarian in their anti-intellectual approach to first principles that they utterly disclaim the doctrine of creation, especially because it is also a divinely revealed truth.

THESIS XVI:

The Corporeal Universe was Created by God.

1. EXPLANATION OF TERMS: Creation means the total production of a thing from nothingness. The being is not produced from itself nor from any presupposed subject. (*Creatio est productio rei ex nihilo sui et subiecti.*)

In modern language we often use the word "creation" metaphorically as in speaking of "creative genius," the "creation of a masterpiece," and that man "creates" new substances by synthetic chemistry.

Creation in the active sense means the action of the Efficient Cause, or creation is considered with respect to God. In the passive sense creation is the dependence of the effect on the Efficient Cause, on God. The thing created is not produced from itself. This is also true in generation—water is not produced from itself but from oxygen and hydrogen in a given proportion. However, in generation the subject of the substantial forms remains in the process; matter remains.

In creation there is a production from nothing in that there is no presupposed subject. This is the specific difference in the definition of creation. The particle "from" does not signify the material cause as if nothing is the subject or matter from which a thing becomes. This particle signifies an order between two terms of change in an improper sense: "before" the thing was not; "now" it is.

The term from which, *terminus a quo*, of creation is nothingness of the whole thing. The term to which, *terminus ad quem*, of creation is the complete and subsisting substance. Hence in the creation of the cosmos neither prime matter nor substantial forms nor accidental forms, properly speaking, were created. They were con-created—they came into being inasmuch as completed substances came into being.

Creation is an instantaneous act because between being and non-being there cannot be a medium. In creation, to become and to be are really the same. The term "becoming" is used in an improper sense, for becoming generally means succession. There is no succession in creation.

"Created by God"—this is said because God is the Supreme Cause.

2. OPPONENTS: All materialists and pantheists.

3. PROOF: *Part* 1:

The universe is either self-sufficient or dependent on another.

And if it is dependent on another, it is so either by production or by emanation from another substance.

But the universe is not-self-sufficient (thesis vs. materialism) nor did it emanate from another, namely the divine substance (thesis vs. pantheism.)

Therefore, the universe has been produced.

But the universe can not be produced from another matter as from a subject.

Therefore, the universe has been produced from nothing, that is to say, it is produced neither from itself nor from any presupposed subject—it has been created.

If the universe were produced from another matter, this matter likewise would have to be produced from another and so on *ad infinitum* which would be an infinite regress of insufficiency in the order of nature. This is repugnant to reason.

PROOF: *Part* 2:

The creator of the universe must be omnipotent.
But God alone is omnipotent.
Therefore, God alone can create the universe.

Major: The Cause that produces something out of nothing, neither from itself nor from any presupposed subject, produces being and consequently the power of such a Cause must extend to all being. The distance, so to speak, between being and non-being is infinite. A power that can bridge the infinite is omnipotent.

Minor: Evident from theodicy that God alone is omnipotent, since He alone is Pure Act.

If the question is asked, whether Aristotle thinks of God as creator of the world, the answer must be certainly that he does not. For him matter is ungenerated, eternal . . . De Caelo 301 b

31, 279 b 12 ff.[1] Although Aristotle has the principles from which the creation of the cosmos can be drawn, he did not draw out this conclusion. It cannot be said that creation really contradicts the Aristotelian philosophy. Aristotle simply did not develop his principles to this conclusion. He knew God as the Prime Mover but not as the Creator.

II. PROBLEMS RELATED TO CREATION

A. CREATION AND TIME. From Plato's *Timaeus*, by way of Philo of Alexandria and the Patristic tradition, the idea that time originated with the universe came into Scholasticism. Before the beginning of the world there was no movement and, therefore, no time. St. Thomas says that St. Augustine is careful to distinguish that the universe was not created in time but with time.[1] According to the Angelic Doctor the beginning of the universe and the beginning of time are simultaneous.

B. CREATION AND THE POSSIBLE ETERNITY OF THE COSMOS. The medieval commentators on Aristotle knew that he held that the heavenly bodies are eternal. In the eighth book of the *Physics* the Stagirite upholds what he falsely believed to be the eternal circular motion of the heavens. Rotary motion, he reasoned, is eternal because in motion of any other kind rest must occur; circular motion is perpetually operative without a starting point, middle or ending point.

There was a great dispute on the subject of the eternity of the cosmos in the Middle Ages. The Arabian philosophers taught the eternity of the world. Moses Maimonides, the leader of Jewish thought in the 12th century, proposed the theory that we can know about creation only through revelation even though some philosophical proofs seem to incline toward the eternity of creation. He had a decisive influence on St. Albert who taught that creation as the absolute positing of being and as a free act of God's will was entirely outside the realm of philosophical proof. St. Albert taught that the world's temporal beginning can be proved once the postulate of creation is admitted.

Although there is disputation concerning the possibility of an eternal cosmos, we know from revelation that the world had

---

[1] W. Ross, *Aristotle* (London: Methuen and Co., 1937), p. 184.
[1] *Contra Gentiles*, Bk. 2, ch. 35.

a beginning *de facto*. The Vatican Council teaches that actually God created from the beginning of time a phrase repeated from the Council of Florence. St. Thomas teaches that the world actually had a beginning, and this is known from revelation.[1] Thus the Christian philosopher admits the actual beginning of the cosmos but the dispute concerns the possibility of an eternal created cosmos.

St. Thomas in his opusculum *On the Eternity of the World* maintains that God could create from all eternity so that a creature could exist which had no temporal beginning of its existence. The argument for the possibility of creation from eternity is that God can create as long as He exists, and He exists from all eternity. The contingency of creatures demands that God must exist before them in the order of nature and not of time.

St. Thomas asserts that it is not impossible "to proceed to infinity accidentally in efficient causes."[2] It is only in the order of necessarily and actually connected causes that we must of necessity arrive at an ultimate cause. St. Thomas cannot see why there should have to be an end to such causes as the hen producing the egg and the egg the hen and so on indefinitely. This is an accidental order of causes.

To carry the series of mobile beings to infinity would not change their nature. As Aristotle remarked, if the world is eternal it is eternally insufficient and incomplete; it eternally demands a sufficient reason for its reality and intelligibility.[3]

C. ENTROPY. The present state of the world insofar as the conditions necessary for life are concerned will eventually come to an end. Scientific induction has established that the amount of energy in the universe is fixed and invariable—this is called the conservation of energy. Amount here is to be understood as the sum total of energy which is available and unavailable. It must be noted that wherever work is done, wherever an energizing condition exists, a certain available energy is lost in diffused heat. Therefore, it is maintained that as useless energy increases, the useful energy decreases by the same amount; this ratio of useless to useful energy is called entropy. The use of the term entropy in this context is to be distinguished from its meaning in thermodynamics.

---

[1] *S. Theol.*, P. 1, q. 46, a. 1 and 2.
[2] *S. Theol.*, P. 1, q. 46, a. 2 and 7.
[3] *Metaph.*, Bk. 12, ch. 6.

Entropy states that the ratio is constantly increasing and this means that the amount of energy available for the energizing process of the world is ever becoming less. Such a decrease means ultimately the end of the conditions necessary for life. Organisms cannot survive except under conditions where considerable energy is available; therefore, organic life will eventually come to an end.

There are other scientists who predict the end of life on the earth in a different way. The Cambridge astronomer, Frederick Hoyle, in his work on *The Nature of the Universe* contends that as more and more hydrogen is converted into helium, the sun will become hotter.[1] By the time the sun has used about a third of its present store of hydrogen the climate of the earth, even at the poles, will be too hot for any forms of life to endure. At a later stage, the oceans will boil and life will be extinct.

These ingenious and fascinating theories are worthy of our consideration. However, it is important to remember that they are theories. Man still knows very little about the future of the universe in its details. We can be certain that at the beginning of the coming century our scientific picture of the end of our world will be different from our present ideas, just as these are different from ideas prevalent at the beginning of our century. It is for these reasons that the philosopher should take care not to make a quite unnecessary defense of the perennial principles of philosophy from our present speculations about the future of our planet and the universe itself.

D. CREATION AND EVOLUTION. There is no repugnance in holding the creation of the cosmos and the mediate formation of the heavens and the earth through natural evolution. God could endow material forms with such powers and activities that they could evolve from some primeval state to other states according to the laws of their natures. Astronomy and geology speculate on how inorganic matter by its powers and activities could have formed the non-living world by a process of evolution. However, it is still disputed as to what were the adequate causes of such a process of evolution. Kant and Laplace independently of each other suggested the hypothesis that the planets and their sat-

---

[1] F Hoyle, *The Nature of the Universe* (N. Y.: Harper Bros., 1950), pp. 74-88.

ellites together with the sun at one time formed a single fiery mass of varying density and that the denser portions became centers of attraction with the result that the entire mass began to rotate and certain parts were separated and formed our planets.

This theory was replaced by the spiral-nebula hypothesis which in turn yielded to the Chamberlain-Moulton theory. This latter conjecture maintains that our planetary system originated in the close approach of another celestial body. The strong attraction set up between the sun and the passing star, attended by internal disturbances within the sun, would cause the eruption of great sections of the sun's substance, which afterwards formed themselves into planets.

Abbé Lemaitre of Louvain advanced another hypothesis which is founded on the expansion of bodies by radioactivity. He views the cosmos as evolving from an original globule, which exploded with such violence that it flung fragments out into space, forming the galaxies of the cosmos. Lemaitre does not insist that it is one original atom that exploded. Since this original disintegration matter has been breaking up into lighter and simpler substances. Lemaitre's cosmos is literally exploding, the farthest galaxies are rushing away at unimaginable speeds.

Frederick Hoyle proposed a new theory in his book entitled *The Nature of the Universe.*[1] It is really the result of developments made by H. Russell, R. Lyttleton and other scientists. Russell had shown that hydrogen is overwhelmingly predominant in the atmospheres of many stars. Hoyle contends that material torn from the sun would not be suitable for the formation of the planets as we know them. The theory, he holds, posits a star moving around the sun that disintegrated with great violence. So great was its explosion that all the remnants were scattered a long way from the sun with the exception of a relatively small mass of gas out of which the earth and other planets have condensed.

The sun held on to this gas and in a few centuries this gas spread out around the sun and took on the form of a rotating circular disk. The temperature of the main bulk of the gas in the disk fell below the freezing point of water. Many kinds of molecules are said to have been generated and these molecules collected into a swarm of solid bodies by a process analogous

[1] F. Hoyle, *op. cit.*, pp. 89-104.

to the formation of water drops in the clouds of our atmosphere. A rough balance between the condensation from gas into solid bodies and evaporation that converted solid matter back into gas then occurred. Hoyle believes that the first condensations to grow large took about 1,000,000,000 years to reach the mass of the earth.

Scientists themselves are not agreed as to the acceptability of any one theory. These hypotheses do not run counter to our cosmology inasmuch as they attempt to assign natural effects to natural causes. Furthermore, these hypotheses attempt to show an ordered progression in nature.

Materialistic philosophies of evolution often claim to be supported by recent scientific attempts to explain the origin of our solar system. The failure to distinguish between hypothesis and fact and between the authority of man as a philosopher and as some sort of special scientist of nature has led to much confusion concerning cosmic evolution. Astronomers such as Haldane and Hoyle are within their field when they discuss the formation of the solar system just as geologists are within their field when they discuss the formation of the earth's surface. But they have wandered from their respective fields as scientists when they approach the problems of the existence of God, creation, and morality. The quest shifts here to the different realms of philosophy and revealed religion.

Hoyle has introduced this type of wandering in the final chapter of his work, *The Nature of the Universe.*[1] In this chapter entitled "A Personal View," although Hoyle cautions the reader that its contents have no agreed basis among the scientists, he plunges into a species of agnosticism which is presented as if blessed with the scientific sanction of his "New Cosmology." He launches out into philosophy in his concept of *continuous creation* There is no attempt made to define terms.

Hoyle's conception of creative evolution in infinite space and time is not a conclusion based on the experimental sciences but rather upon a pseudo-philosophy of nature. The use of the term *creative* in this context applies to Hoyle's concept of created material which simply appears from nowhere. There is no foundation in reality presented for this assumption in Hoyle's universe either in terms of primary or secondary causality. How-

[1] F. Hoyle, *op. cit.,* pp. 133-142.

ever, many readers of Hoyle's work will fail to evaluate his pseudo-philosophy of nature as distinct in its object and method from his work as a theorist in cosmogony. In this later capacity Hoyle is certainly noteworthy.

Whether the cosmos evolved from some other state than that in which it now exists or not in no way destroys the nature of the cosmos as a mutable, finite, contingent and multiple entity which is not-self-sufficient. The specialists in astronomy, geology and other such sciences of nature cogitate upon the created cosmos of mobile beings whose evolution they seek to explain scientifically. Hence, their object is not to explain its mobile being as mobile but rather its becoming in a flux of forms according to their secondary principles. The order of the sciences must be observed in respect to their objects and methods.

E. THE ANTI-PROTON AND "THE ANNIHILTAION OF MATTER." Since God alone can create, God alone can annihilate. But for God to annihilate would not be in accordance with His wisdom and goodness as St. Thomas explains:

> Some of the things which God does in creatures occur in accordance with the natural course of things; others happen miraculously.... those things which happen miraculously are ordered to the manifestations of grace.... The nature of things show that none of them is annihilated. For either they are immaterial and therefore have no potentiality to non-being or they are material and then they continue to exist, at least in matter, which is incorruptible since it is the subject of a generation and corruption. Moreover, the annihilation of things does not pertain to the manifestation of grace since the power and goodness of God are rather manifested by the conservation of things in being. Therefore we must conclude by denying absolutely that anything at all will be annihilated.[1]

In 1956 it was publicly announced that a University of California laboratory had produced a remarkable new atomic particle, the anti-proton, which can annihilate the basic building block of all matter. *Annihilation of matter* is not to be understood as the real meaning of this report. What is to be understood is a transformation of mass into energy. According to a theory originated by P. A. M. Dirac each type of particle (electrons, protons, neutrons) has a mate, an anti-particle. If an

---

[1] S Theol., P. 1, q. 104, a. 4.

electron and a positron collide, they are both "annihilated," i.e., they both disappear and a photon (X ray particle) appears.

Similarly if a proton obeys Dirac's theory, there should be an anti-proton or negatively charged proton in nature. The particle accelerator at the University of California can accelerate protons to energies of about six billion electron volts. A beam of these protons was directed on a copper target and the particles coming off were analyzed as to mass and charge. The "annihilation radiation" was also observed. The anti-protons produced apparently collided with ordinary protons, each disappearing and their mass being converted into energy. In the strict sense, there was no annihilation of matter, a reduction to nothing, but rather a transformation. The use of terms by the physicist must be properly understood.

Suggested Reading

Aristotle, *Physics*, Bk. 8, ch. 6, *op. cit.*
St. Thomas Aquinas, *Summa Theologica* P. 1, q. 45; P. 1, q. 46, a. 2, ad 7; *Quodlibeta*, no. 12, q. 2.
R. Garrigou-LaGrange, *God: His Existence and His Nature* (St. Louis: Herder Co., 1934), p. 77 and ff.
E. Gilson, *The Philosophy of St. Thomas Aquinas* (St. Louis: Herder Co., 1939), pp. 132-166.
J. Jean. *Astronomy and Cosmogony* (Cambridge, England: The University Press, 1928).
G. Duggan, *Evolution and Philosophy* (New Zealand: A. H. & A. W. Reed, 1949).

Questions

1. State the thesis on creation.
    a. Define the terms of the thesis.
    b. Prove the thesis in form.
2. When Aristotle speaks of the Unmoved First Mover does he mean the Creator? How are his principles on this subject related to the teaching of St. Thomas on God the Creator?
3. Was the universe created in time or with time? Explain your answer.
4. What is meant by the problem of the eternity of the cosmos as it is treated by the medieval masters? What is St. Thomas' teaching on the eternity of the cosmos.
5. What is meant by entropy?
6. Write an essay on creation and evolution. Consider the following in your essay:
    a. The proper relation of the scientific theories of evolution to the philosophical doctrine of creation.
    b. Modern scientific theories on the evolution of our cosmos.
    c. The popular fallacy of the uniform method in the evaluation of evolutionary theories.
7. Can mobile being be annihilated? Prove your answer.

Section 2

The Final Cause of Mobile Being: The Glory of God

THE VERY EXISTENCE of the sciences testifies that the universe is worthy of study in the light of principles and causes. It is a cosmos, an orderly arrangement. We have studied this order of nature from the aspect of the intrinsic causes of mobile being itself and the Supreme Efficient Cause of mobile being. There remains for us to explore the problem of the final cause of mobile being as it is rendered intelligible in the destiny of the cosmos, in the ultimate reason for mobile being.

This study in finality involves a series of fundamental problems. Does nature act for an end? Or is it that our thinking makes it so? Do we really live in a whirl of uncertainties? If nature acts for an end, is the end intended? Is it known and freely willed? How do the mobile beings of the cosmos tend to an end? Are they drawn through a motion purely from without or by reason of their very natures which incline to specific ends? What is the ultimate end of all the specific secondary ends of mobile beings?

These are the problems which occupy us in this final section of the course. They pertain to the most important cause of the cosmos, the destiny, the reason for its being at all. There is a fundamental *why* in the inquiring mind of every man: why is the universe existing? Man naturally seeks to render the cosmos intelligible in its destiny not only because man is a rational animal but also because the cosmos is intelligible. Intelligence Itself made its total being.

It must be noted that we are dealing here with universal finality and not with particular and special ends as such. The latter should be studied in physics, chemistry, biology and the other special sciences. These disciplines ought to investigate the special finalities of mobile beings, and their utility as related to man and the universe.

We shall see that finality in nature is under attack by almost every system of modern thought. We shall endeavor to explain this trend.

The Purposive Finality of Mobile Being and the Physical Laws

I. PURPOSIVE FINALITY

THESIS XVII:

Mobile Beings Tend to an End Through an Innate Tendency. There is in the Material Universe a Purposive Finality.

1. MEANING OF THE THESIS: We do not affirm that all mobile beings act formally toward an end, that is, as if endowed with intelligence as the hylozoists maintain. But we say there is in all things of nature an inclination whereby they follow a determined good intended by the Supreme Being.

2. EXPLANATION OF TERMS: "End" or "final cause" is that for the sake of which a thing is done. A final cause does not exclude an efficient cause. The efficient cause is that cause which produces an effect by its own physical activity. A man working in an office is the efficient cause of his work, but there is evidently

another extrinsic cause here, namely, his wages. The man produces the work and his work is produced because of the wages. The final cause induces the efficient cause to act and directs the action along definite lines. It is the goal that moves the efficient cause. To tend toward an end means to have an inclination and direction for obtaining a determined good.

The inclination toward an end is called *perfect* or *formal* when an agent knows an intended end and the suitable means, e.g. man is such an agent. The inclination toward an end is called *imperfect* or *material* when an agent tends to an end known and freely willed not by the being itself but by some intelligent agent. This is the inclination, or natural appetite of the inorganic, vegetative and animal orders. It is applied to inorganic and vegetable beings incapable of any cognition whatever. It is also true of the natural appetites of animals because their sensitive appetite does not know an end as an end as related to suitable means. They simply tend to the end they naturally apprehend. Bees do not comprehend solid geometry, but they construct their hives with geometrical precision precisely because they are bees. We shall see that God is the Intelligent Agent Who knows and freely wills all natural appetites. It should be noted that we do not rest the case by saying "it is the will of God," a current Communist objection against finality in nature.

Intrinsic finality is an inclination in a mobile being itself, and through which inclination a mobile being tends to a good convenient to it. Thus trees are inclined to grow toward light. *Extrinsic* finality is the appropriation of a being to the good of another; as wheat for bread and bread for man. The *intrinsic* good of one being is the *extrinsic* good of some other being.

By an *innate tendency* we mean through an intrinsic form which is permanent in a mobile being. This form is the principle by which a mobile being tends to an end. Remotely, it is the determined nature or principle of activity of a mobile being. Proximately, it is the powers or faculties derived from the nature of a being. For example, spiders build webs for shelter and as traps for food because it is their nature to do so. They are inclined to this end remotely by their kind of substantial form and proximately by the inclination to spin designs which is in their tiny organs called spinnerets directed by their instinct.

By *order* we mean the harmonious cooperation of many members to the same end. As applied to the universe it means that the different appetites or affinities of the mobile beings of the universe are such as to produce a continuous series of ordered events. This series of events is known as the order of the course of nature. The advance of the natural sciences has revealed the wonderful interrelation and mutual cooperation of the parts of the material universe all the way from the subatomic particles to the celestial bodies.

By *purposive finality* is meant a finality that is intended by an intelligent agent. It is asserted that mobile beings possess finality by reason of purpose in the mind of an Intelligent Cause. Hence, they are not ordered to ends by chance or blind necessity.

3. OPPONENTS: Certain mechanists, Democritus among them, said that the course of nature is purely fortuitous. The materialistic monists, the fatalists, and the pantheists deny that the order of the world is intended by an Intelligent Author of nature. Some, like Kant, hold that finality is purely subjective. Others such as Francis Bacon and Descartes held that finality should not be investigated, that it is not a scientific question. Francis Bacon wrote: "The habit of seeking final causes in physics has expelled and, as it were, banished from it the physical causes ... "[1]

4. PROOF: *Part* 1:

What acts, tends towards an end.
But mobile beings act.
Therefore, mobile beings tend to an end.

Major: Whatever acts, produces something determined. But if the effect is determined, the action is itself determined. But if the action is determined, it tends necessarily to a determined end. For example, hydrogen and oxygen in a determined proportion necessarily tend to produce a determined effect, water. This process is determined toward producing the end, water.

The anti-finalist says that we have H_2O because we have H and O in a certain proportion, but we do not have H and O uniting in a certain proportion in order to have H_2O. We see because we have eyes, the anti-finalist argues; we do not have

---

[1] De dim. et. augm. scien., III, 4.

eyes in order to see. Such an argument fails to grasp the relation between a determined action and a determined end. It restricts the determination of action to one direction, the source, and neglects the determination to the goal. It restricts causality to the action of efficient causality as if efficient causality were in contradiction instead of contrariety to final causality.

Minor: Evident from the thesis on qualities.

PROOF: *Part 2*:

Mobile beings tend to an end through an innate tendency, if they act through principles (nature and qualities) internal and determined in them.

But mobile beings act through principles internal and determined in them.

Therefore, mobile beings tend to an end through an innate tendency.

Major: Evident from the definition of an innate tendency.

Minor: A mobile being tends to an end either purely through extrinsic motion or through an innate tendency. But mobile being does not tend to an end purely through extrinsic motion. Therefore, it tends to an end through an innate tendency. If mobile beings tend to an end only because they are moved from without, then they would cease to conserve a tendency to an end when the extrinsic cause ceases. But mobile beings do conserve such a tendency. Thus one element retains an affinity for a certain other element even if the latter is not present.

PROOF: *Part 3*:

Observation of the material universe reveals a constant and wonderful order.

But where there is a constant and wonderful order there is purposive finality.

Therefore, there is in the material universe a purposive finality.

Major: Experience and the natural sciences reveal a constant and wonderful order in the material universe. It suffices to mention here the three grand divisions of mobile beings that cooperate toward the good of the universe in general. The inorganic kingdom is fitted to serve life on earth in some way.

Plants together with inorganic substances minister to animal life and all these lesser beings serve man.

This cooperation of the mobile beings of the universe toward the perfection of the whole was grasped by the ancient Greeks, and so they named the universe "the cosmos," a thing of beauty, a wonderful order. In the course of man's history on earth he has come to know more and more of that order. This knowledge, as it became more and more refined and detailed, gave rise to the special sciences of physics, chemistry, mineralogy and the rest. Their systems of principles report the objective order in the world around us.

Minor: A constant and wonderful order could not be without intention. If a constant and wonderful order could exist without intention, then it would exist by chance or by an absolute blind necessity. But a constant order cannot exist by chance and a wonderful order cannot be by absolute blind necessity.

a) Constant order is not casual. What happens casually is not stable and uniform. But natural agents act in a stable and uniform manner. Hence, the order of nature cannot be called casual.

b) The wonderful order of the universe is not by a blind and absolute necessity. What exists by blind necessity does not arise by wonderful selection of means to an end, which manifests the work of intelligence instead of blindness because of the essential relation between fitness and intention. The imperfect does not give rise to the perfect. Just as the discovery of tools on a lone island reveals that these were the products of intelligence, so, too, the marvelous order of nature reveals an Intelligent Cause of the nature of things.

When a being exists by absolute necessity, it is absolutely repugnant that it exist in any other way. But the order manifest in the universe could be conceived absolutely otherwise than it is—the orbits of the planets in general could be larger or smaller, the climate of the earth could be otherwise than it is. But absolute necessity negates any other possibility as it is absolutely impossible that a circle be a square. Such necessity does not fit the order of nature in general. We shall return to this in thesis XVIII. We have touched upon the ultimate reason for finality, a Supreme Intelligence; it remains for theodicy to develop these premises in the teleological proof for the existence of God. Such development is not proper to the science of cosmology.

A. THE CHARGE OF ANTHROPOMORPHISM. Anti-finalists often charge finalists with anthropomorphism, that the finalist is reading into nature the purposiveness of human activity. But the Thomist is careful to distinguish between material and formal finality. He teaches that man alone in the corporeal universe seeks his end rationally.[1] Lower beings have of themselves no purpose in their action. Animals do not know their purpose in acting, stones have no intention in falling.

The Thomist is careful to distinguish direction toward an end in different senses as it is applied to man, animal, plant and mineral. Man acts for an end with knowledge of purpose, and he is able to choose his means. Animals act for an end with sense knowledge of the thing for which they act, but not knowing their purpose. Plants and inorganic substances act for an end insofar as they act definitely and uniformly for something. Such action is determined for them by the laws of their natures according to the intentions of the Creator.

Those who advance the charge of anthropomorphism against the thesis on finality in the cosmos propose to argue against a statement on cosmic finality which they have conceived. They view it in terms of man imposing his intentions on the world. It is against this straw theory that they so brilliantly argue. There is great need for more direct communication between Thomists and their modern critics.

B. DARWINISM AND FINALITY. The theory of natural selection by the survival of the fittest which Charles Darwin maintained in his work, *The Origin of Species by Means of Natural Selection* (1859), attempts to explain species by a fortuitous cumulation of variations. Strange as it may seem, Aristotle was aware of such a doctrine which he ascribes to Empedocles.[2] We read in *Physics* II, 8; 19b:

> Similarly, if a man's crop is spoiled on the threshing floor, the rain did not fall for the sake of this—in order that the crop might be spoiled—but that result just followed. Why then should not it be the same with the parts of nature, e.g. that our teeth should come up of

[1] In 2 *Physics*, lects. 13 and 14.
[2] Fragment 61, 2.

necessity—the front teeth sharp, fitted for tearing, the molars broad and useful for grinding down the food—since they did not arise with this end, but it was merely a coincident result; and so with all other parts in which we suppose that there is purpose? Wherever then all the parts came about just what they would have been if they had come to be for an end, such things *survived*, being organized spontaneously *in a fitting way;* whereas those which grew otherwise perished and continue to perish, as Empedocles says his "man-faced ox-progeny did."

Aristotle answers this argument in the following passage in the *Physics* II, 8; 198b, 199a:

Yet it is impossible that this should be the true view. For teeth and all other natural things either invariably or normally come about in a given way; but of not one of the results of chance or of spontaneity is this true. We do not ascribe to chance or mere coincidence the frequency of rain in winter, but frequent rain in summer we do; nor heat in the dog-days, but only if we have it in winter. If then, it is agreed that things are either the result of coincidence or for an end and these cannot be the result of coincidence or spontaneity, it follows that they must be for an end . . .

Darwinian evolution, just as ancient casualism, does not explain permanence of types in nature, that animals breed true to type and rarely produce monstrosities. Actually this theory states that some things are fitted to survive; hence it is implied that they are adapted to the end which is "survival."

The denial of finality means the denial of definite natures in things and, therefore, definite modes of action—a denial consistent neither with reason nor experience. Furthermore, the very concept of chance itself supposes law. For if there is no rule there can be no exception; to say that everything is by chance is to deny chance.

It is important to note that the philosopher in pleading the case of finality in nature is not taking on the impossible task of denoting the particular ends of each being in nature. It suffices for the philosopher to assert that every being acts for an end (*Omne ens agit propter finem*) in his universal study of the nature of things.[1] It is for the experimental scientist to reveal the particular ends of the various classes of mobile beings and their use to man.

---

[1] *Contra. Gentiles,* Bk. 3, ch. 2.

II. NECESSITY AND FINALITY

THESIS XVIII:

*The Activities of Mobile Beings of Nature are Governed
by Physical Laws of Hypothetical Necessity.*

1. MEANING OF THE THESIS: We do not treat of natural moral law
or man as a free-agent in this thesis but of the physical laws
of nature. These concern intrinsic inclinations of mobile beings
toward determined modes of action. Such laws exist independently of the human mind. We affirm in this thesis that physical
laws concerning the activities of mobile beings depend on the
free intention of God; they have only hypothetical necessity.

2. EXPLANATION OF TERMS: The *mobile beings of nature* refer
to all objects that occur in nature without interference on the
part of man. Thus we exclude artificial entities such as machines
and engineering achievements in general.

The *physical laws are necessary*: Given the determined
nature of a mobile being and conditions required for its activities
they follow in a determined way. We say that the necessity
of the physical laws are hypothetical or conditional because
their operation in their determined mode depends on the condition that God does not prevent the natural phenomenon from
taking place. God can suspend the necessity which rules the
course of nature.

3. OPPONENTS: All professed atheists, as the followers of Karl
Marx. All determinists, who hold that the physical laws have
absolute necessity. All who profess indeterminism, Henri Bergson, Maurice Blondel, Werner Heisenberg—these thinkers assert
that each phenomenon is a singular case and demands a unique
solution. Agnostics and positivists who say that physical laws are
only symbols of the real and that we know only successions of
phenomena and not causality itself.

4. PROOF: *Part 1*:

If mobile beings act according to a constant mode, they are
acting according to a stable norm or law necessarily determined.

But mobile beings act according to a constant mode.

Therefore, there are physical laws which are necessary.

Major: Evident from the notion of physical laws.

Minor: Evident from the preceding thesis.

PROOF: *Part 2:*

The necessity which governs the phenomena of the corporeal universe is only hypothetical and not absolute. If granted all the material conditions requisite for the phenomena to occur its occurrence is still contingent on the power of the Creator.

But such is the case.

Therefore, the necessity which governs the phenomena of the corporeal universe is hypothetical.

Major: Metaphysical necessity or absolute necessity pertains to things in their intrinsic constitution, essences which are internally immutable. Hence, by no reason and by no cause can a man not be a rational animal. If the necessity with which physical agents act can be annulled by God, it is only hypothetical.

Minor: No creature can act without the concurrent power of God, because it is contingent in its activity as well as in its being, and God is not bound to give that concurrence. If He were bound, He would be subject to the creature He has made. God is supremely independent of any being distinct from Himself.

The Creator Who, without any created agent, originally produced mobile being can, without employing any such agent, impede the action of the agents of the corporeal universe, heighten or lessen their power or direct them to other than their connatural objects. All this God can do without undoing the nature of mobile being. It is to be noted that properties flow from the nature of a thing, but they do not constitute its nature or essence. Consequently God can suspend actions proper to a being without destroying its essence.

III. THE HEISENBERG PRINCIPLE OF UNCERTAINTY

In recent times much speculation has been aroused by the principle of indeterminism (or uncertainty) as formulated by Werner Heisenberg.[1] Imagine that an electron is moving rapidly through some sort of an apparatus in the laboratory. As it passes

---

[1] W. Heisenberg, *Philosophic Implication of Nuclear Science* (New York: Pantheon, 1952).

a particular point the observer wishes to determine its position and velocity. The electron is too small to disturb the long wave lengths of visible light and, if observed at all, must be illumined with the very short waves of the gamma radiation. But a gamma-ray photon has a great deal of energy, much more than that of a photon of visible light because its frequency is greater. The gamma-ray photon must strike the electron in order to reveal the electron's presence. But when it does, the large energy and mass of the photon is too much for the feeble electron, which may be knocked completely out of the apparatus. The operation of observing the electron has so altered its velocity that it is impossible to gain any idea as to what velocity the electron really has.

It appears that one can measure either the position of an electron or its velocity but not both at the same time if great accuracy is desired. According to the modern view, electrons are observable statistically but not individually when simultaneous determination of position and velocity is desired. From this some contemporary physicists such as Heisenberg maintain that the law of causality no longer applies to nature. Nature is indeterminate; hence, our thesis concerning the physical laws of nature is regarded by them as scientifically meaningless. Heisenberg himself believes that the restoration of determinism in nature would destroy quantum mechanics. On the other hand, Planck and Einstein have maintained that the indeterminism of which the Heisenberg principle speaks is an inexactitude in our knowledge of nature, and therefore a temporary barrier which will pass.

The indeterminacy of the Heisenberg principle is true of the mind measuring. It describes the limitations of our judgment regarding the behavior of the individual electron. What it says is true of the measuring power of the mind according to the present state of its knowledge concerning this phenomenon. But this is not the same as saying that the individual electron is itself indeterminate. There is a difference between the inexactitude of our knowledge and the indeterminism of nature.

The indeterminacy of the Heisenberg principle is an indeterminacy of knowledge in a new field in which methods are still being tested and new experimentation is in preparation. The exaggeration of the importance of the Heisenberg principle stems from a false appreciation of the method of physics—as if the measurements of the physicist speak the final word on mobile reality, in which case physics would supplant the philosophy of nature. It is a case of over-emphasis of the role of the mind as measuring in science.

IV. ORDER AND THE COURSE OF NATURE

By the *course* of nature is understood the sequence of events. The *order* of nature is the local arrangement in which the various mobile beings in the universe are placed with respect to each other at any given moment. The order of nature in the beginning of things must be ascribed to the Creator alone; the subsequent orders of nature, except where interfered with by the arbitrary intervention of man or of God, are due to the workings of natural agents according to the divinely instituted course of such agents.

V. THE UNIFORMITY OF NATURE

Under certain suitable conditions, there is uniformity in the activity of mobile beings. All the natural sciences are built upon the recognition of this uniformity. It must be understood that this uniformity of nature is the effect of law. The expression of this uniformity in mathematical symbols, for example $F=kma$, is sometimes called a law.

Law, however, properly speaking, includes in its concept a superior and a subject. Strictly speaking, the subjects of law are rational creatures. For only rational creatures can be obliged by a rule.[1] It is only by analogy, therefore, that we speak of law in non-intelligent creatures inasmuch as there is a rule of operation in them according to which they act or do not act. It is in this sense that we spoke of law in the preceding thesis. It is a concept of law analagously understood by the philosopher.

The experimental scientist is concerned with how events happen rather than with the universal "why" of things. From observation and analysis he arrives at certain functional relations of mobility expressed in a mathematical formula which describes certain uniformity of events. This is a physical law in an empirological sense of the term. But uniformity is actually

---

[1] *S. Theol.* P. 1-2, q. 91, a. 2.

the result of physical law in the strict sense, as uniform functions suppose the uniform inclinations of powers which are fixed according to the mobile being's nature.

The empiricist who will not go beyond the functional relations, therefore, never comes to the basic concept of physical law. He describes uniformity but he fails to understand its roots in the nature of the mobile beings concerned. Empiricism denies the existence of objective qualities and natures. It cannot explain the uniformity of nature objectively, and sometimes oversimplifies the explanation of our scientific knowledge of the world by attributing it to mental symbolism, an inferential process of the mind. In contemporary America it is particularly evidenced in what is called *logical empiricism* as represented in the writings of Philipp Frank of Harvard University.[1] This empiricism has had a tremendous influence in English speaking countries since the mass exodus of logical empiricists to the United States after the Anschluss of 1938.

The laws of the experimental scientist do not state the causes of changes, because they do not hunt in this field of inquiry. They express quantitative relations of qualities of the mobile. Let us take for example the law: "Bodies attract in direct proportion to their masses and in inverse proportion to the square of their distances of separation." At first glance it would seem that the scientist is speaking of the force called attraction in terms of a cause of movement. But a little reflection shows us that it is not so. By force the scientist does not mean the efficient cause but a mathematical measure of mass and acceleration. This law, therefore, formally concerns the constant and uniform relation which unites the acceleration of bodies, their masses and distances. Such relations are in some mode connected with the formal cause of a mobile being. On the part of the mind they approximate rather than report with precision the quantitative relations of qualities of the mobile; they are ever open to correction.

Suggested Reading

Aristotle, *Physics* Bks. 1, 2, *op. cit.*
St. Thomas Aquinas, *Contra Gentiles*, Bk. 3, ch. 2; *Summa Theo-*

---

[1] Philipp Frank, *Modern Science and Its Philosophy*, (Cambridge, Mass.: Harvard University Press, 1949), pp. 277-280.

logica P. 2-2, q. 1, a. 2; P. 1, 44. a. 4.; *In 2 Physics,* lects. 13, 14, 15.

R. Garrigou-LaGrange, *God: His Existence and His Nature, op. cit.* Vol. I, pp. 362-366.

V. Smith, *Philosophical Physics* (New York: Harper and Bros., 1950), pp. 268-270.

D. Bohm, *Causality and Chance in Modern Physics,* (London, Routledge and Kegan Paul, 1958)

Questions

1. State the thesis on finality in the cosmos.
   a. What is the meaning of the thesis?
   b. Define the terms.
   c. Who are the opponents?
   d. Prove the thesis.
2. What is meant by the charge of anthropomorphism against this thesis? How would you answer this charge?
3. What ancient error does Darwinian evolution repeat concerning final causes? How would you evaluate this theory?
4. State the thesis on the necessity of the physical laws.
   a. What is the meaning of the thesis?
   b. Define the terms.
   c. Who are the opponents?
   d. Prove the thesis.
5. Criticize the Heisenberg principle of uncertainty as it is used by the indeterminists.
6. Define and explain the terms: order of nature, course of nature, uniformity of nature.
7. Write an essay on the meaning of physical laws in experimental science. Illustrate your principles by some physical law used in experimental science.

The Possibility of Miracles

I. Introduction.
II. Thesis 19: Miracles are Possible.
III. Classification of Miracles.
IV. Miracles are not against Nature.

I. INTRODUCTION

THE WORD "MIRACLE" is perhaps one of the most misused terms of modern times. Along with such terms as "the supernatural," "mysticism," and "spirit," it is often associated with magic or with the occult. The fad of agnosticism, particularly in the last century, contributed much toward distorting the meaning of miracle. Since miracles are beyond the powers of nature, the agnostic supposes that they are impossible. Voltaire in the age of the so-called "Enlightenment" wrote:

> A miracle is the violation of mathematical, divine, immutable and eternal laws. By this very statement a miracle is a contradiction in terms, a law cannot be at the same time immutable and violated.[1]

The literary Matthew Arnold was of the opinion that the trouble with miracles is that they never happen.

Nowadays as a reaction to the classical determinism of the last century, the indeterminism of some men of science affirms that every new emergent in the evolutionary process is "miraculous." Whitehead speaks of reality as a constant creative advance into novelty. The pendulum has thus swung to the other extreme. The universe is considered by these thinkers to be devoid of absolutely necessary laws and is viewed as a purely contingent process, an ever unfolding series of novelties.

This indeterminism evokes pessimism in the existentialism of Jean Paul Sartre. He writes that:

---

[1] F. Voltaire, *Dictionnaire Philosophique* (Londres, 1765).

... for the existentialist man the objective universe is only a cause of vexation, which nothing can be done about, indifferent at heart, a perpetual state of the probable....[1]

For Sartre such a universe is anything but miraculous; it is nauseating.

Modern critics of the miraculous are accustomed to follow in the line of Voltaire's critique that a miracle is a violation of the immutable laws of nature. Notwithstanding the indeterminism current in modern thought, objections to the miraculous are often found in the view that nature is determined by laws closed to any superior agent. For example, Einstein in his work: *The World as I See It,* wrote:

> The man who is thoroughly convinced of the universal operation of the law of causation cannot for a moment entertain the idea of a being who interferes in the course of events—that is, if he takes the hypothesis of causality really seriously.[2]

Max Planck in his *Scientific Autobiography and Other Papers* maintains the similar belief:

> The faith in miracles must yield ground, step by step, before the steady and firm advance of the forces of science, and its total defeat is indubitably a mere matter of time. The younger generation of our own era, which in any case is sharply critical toward traditional views, no longer permits itself to be bound by doctrines which it regards as contradictory to the laws of nature.[3]

Recently a popular work entitled *Worlds in Collision* by Immanuel Velikovsky has attempted to explain certain miraculous phenomena such as the rain of manna for the Israelites in the desert as rare but natural phenomena.[4] Works such as this manifest an ever recurrent attempt to naturalize the miraculous. Although Velikovsky's explanations were rejected by men of science, the assumption that the natural can explain away the miraculous was not included amongst the errors cited.

---

[1] Jean Paul Sartre, *Existentialism* (New York: Philosophical Library, 1947), p. 81.
[2] Albert Einstein, *The World as I See It* (New York: Philosophical Library, 1949) p. 27.
[3] M. Planck, *Scientific Autobiography and Other Papers* (New York: Philosophical Library, 1949), p. 155.
[4] I. Velikovsky, *Worlds in Collision* (New York: Macmillan Co., 1950).

In the following thesis we shall examine the alleged contradiction between natural laws and miracles on the part of God. It should be already clear from the preceding thesis that the laws of nature are not closed to the intervention of God, since they are not absolutely necessary laws. Einstein and Planck along with many other critics of the miraculous assume that the laws of nature are not open to the intervention of a Superior Agent. They neglect to examine the grades of necessity and prefer to judge reality solely from the limited viewpoint of the new physics.

II. THESIS XIX:

MIRACLES ARE POSSIBLE

1. MEANING OF THE THESIS: It is to be noted that the present thesis is not repetitious of the preceding one. The latter states that the necessity of nature's laws is hypothetical; God can intervene in the course of nature. In the present thesis we assert that miracles are possible because nature is open to divine intervention and such intervention does not contradict the divine attributes, especially God's immutability and wisdom.

2. EXPLANATION OF TERMS: A miracle is defined as a perceptible event which is an exception to the course of nature and effected by divine intervention. By "perceptible" is meant an object of sense perception such as a cure at Lourdes which can be perceived in its effects.

By "an exception to the course of nature" is meant that, given the natural conditions, the natural agents could not effect the event. It is outside the course of nature (*praeter naturam*). For example, Lourdes water, which is physically simply H_2O, cannot of itself cure cancer.

"Effected by divine intervention" means that God alone is the principal cause of a miracle. He may use man as an instrumental cause as when Moses was used by God to strike a rock and water gushed forth. It is to be noted that man also intervenes in nature but he does not change the course of nature in doing so. Natural agents employed in the service of man still act according to their inclinations under suitable conditions. Man disposes these toward ends useful in some way to himself such as in engineering pursuits, for example, the construction of levees against floods. Man cannot suspend the physical necessity which rules the activity of natural agents, for God alone as Author of nature can do this. In doing so, God need not abrogate the law which is given in the natural agent, for the innate tendency may still remain although void of its proper effect.

By "possible" we mean that it is adequately possible—intrinsically and extrinsically there is no contradiction in a miracle; neither in its notion nor in its existence.

3. Opponents: All professed atheists and the so-called rationalists. Ernest Renan, (1823-1892) David Strauss (1808-1874) and Adolph Harnack (1851-1930) are among the representative "rationalists." They argue that it would be imperfect of God if He would interfere in the course of nature.

4. proof:

Miracles are possible if there is nothing on the part of the physical laws of the corporeal universe or on the part of God to make them impossible.

But on neither account is there anything to render them impossible.

Therefore, miracles are possible.

Major: Evident from the notion of miracle.

Minor: The preceding thesis has shown that the physical laws are only hypothetically necessary, and so they cannot be opposed to intervention on the part of the Creator. On the part of God there is nothing to prevent His freely interfering with the course of nature. As our adversaries admit, the two attributes of God concerned are His immutability and His wisdom. But His immutability does not prevent Him from making exceptions in the course of nature. God does not change His plan but from eternity decrees laws and exceptions to laws. Nor is this against His wisdom because by miracles God is not correcting His laws but is acting for a higher good for His creatures, for example, an expression of His Love for them or an authorization of some teaching as coming from Him. This subject is studied at length in Apologetics.

III. CLASSIFICATION OF MIRACLES

An event may be outside the power of nature in three ways: with respect to *substance, subject,* and *mode* or manner. The *substance* of the event is beyond nature when nature simply cannot produce the effect at all, such as the conversion of water into wine. The miracle is said to be one of *subject* when nature can produce the effect but not in the given subject, e.g., restoring life to a dead body. A miracle is one of *mode* or manner when nature can produce the effect but not in the way given, e.g., immediate cessation of a storm at sea.

IV. MIRACLES ARE NOT AGAINST NATURE

Strictly speaking, miracles are not against nature, for all things are naturally subjected to God. The First Cause subjects them to His Power in a special way in order to cause some effect beyond the power of the natural agent concerned.

We may distinguish three orders in nature: a *particular* order such as the order of the stars in the heavens, the *universal* order of all mobile beings which includes all the powers of the cosmos and the *most universal* order of divine providence. This latter pertains to nature in whatever way it is ordered by God. A miracle is beyond the particular order of mobile beings concerned; for example, the cure of cancer by Lourdes water is beyond the power of the water itself and it is beyond the universal order of mobile beings in that no natural cause or causes can explain the miraculous effects at Lourdes, but it is not beyond the most universal order of divine providence. This order contains the reason why a miracle, an exception to the natural order, occurs.

Cosmology as a study of nature by the light of natural reason simply explains the possibility of miracles in the universe. It establishes the important truth that we live in a world open to the possibility of extraordinary sensible divine facts. The hypothetical necessity of natural laws and the nature of God and His attributes show no repugnance to miraculous phenomena. The dogmatism of modern sceptics, who have convinced themselves that the miraculous never can happen, is repugnant to sound reason.

Suggested Reading

St. Thomas Aquinas, *Summa Theologica*, P. 1, q. 105, arts. 6-8; *Contra Gentiles*, Bk. 3, chs. 98-104.

J. H. Newman. *Two Essays on Miracles* (London: Longmans, Green and Co., 1918).

J. Driscoll. "Miracle" in *The Catholic Encyclopedia*, Vol. X.

Questions

1. Define "miracle" and explain the terms of the definition.
2. Who are some modern opponents of the possibility of miracles? What reasons do they give for their opposition?
3. Prove that miracles are possible.
4. Enumerate the kinds of miracles.
5. Explain what is meant by the proposition: miracles are not against nature. How do we identify miracles in the three orders in nature?

CHAPTER III

The Ultimate End of the Universe

I. THE GLORY OF GOD: THE END OF THE UNIVERSE

THERE ARE FINAL causes which lead on to further final causes. We know that there is in the corporeal universe an ascending scale of purposes. Some are proximate, others are remote; and in each series of related ends one final cause is ultimate. The ultimate end of any series is that which gives meaning to the whole series.

For example, the perfection of the planet Earth is the relatively ultimate end of the physical substances that are united in its being. This end is ultimate in a certain respect, namely, in respect to this planet. The mineral, vegetable and animal kingdoms all serve in some way to perfect the earth, which serves as the abode of man. It is only when other ends lead to a certain end that we can speak of the latter as relatively ultimate in respect to a series of ends.

All series of ends with their relatively ultimate ends tend toward an end which is absolutely ultimate. It is this absolutely ultimate end that we consider in the following thesis.

THESIS XX:

The Absolutely Ultimate, Extrinsic End of the Universe is the Glory of God

1. MEANING OF THE THESIS: This thesis asserts that there is a destiny for the universe itself and this is found only in the glory of God.

2. EXPLANATION OF TERMS: The meaning of *absolutely ultimate end* as opposed to a relatively ultimate end has been explained. We speak of an *extrinsic end* because the absolutely ultimate end is really distinct from the universe. By *glory* we mean *clear knowledge with praise.* It signifies adequate recognition and appreciation. We glorify a person when we recognize his excellence and praise him because of it.

There are two ways in which glory can be understood, namely, objectively and formally. By *objective* glory is meant the excellence of the thing—thus the universe is the objective glory of God in that it manifests His excellence. It is an analogous participation in the perfection of God. *Formal* glory means the knowledge of this excellence with praiseful appreciation.

In this thesis we are speaking of the glory of God as the natural destiny of creatures. Formally, this means the knowledge, love and praise which His rational creatures give to Him on account of the excellence of His creation which manifests His Goodness. Objectively, this glory consists in His admirably fashioned creatures, the order of the universe, the beauty of nature which *reflect* His Goodness.

3. OPPONENTS: All professed atheists and agnostics: all those who regard the universe as a meaningless process or who seek to explain it totally by itself without any reference to a Supreme Being, Who is really distinct from the universe.

4. PROOF:

The absolutely ultimate extrinsic end of the universe is that on account of which all mobile beings exist and act.

But all mobile beings exist and act for the glory of God.

Therefore, the absolutely ultimate extrinsic end of the universe is the glory of God.

Major: The absolutely ultimate extrinsic end is distinguished from a proximate particular end. The former is attributed to all mobile beings; the latter, to some mobile beings. In the cosmic order of finality proximate ends lead to the absolutely ultimate extrinsic end. Otherwise, the finite intermediary ends would be without sufficient reason. Finite contingent reality is neither its own first efficient cause nor its absolutely ultimate end.

Minor: God alone is the absolutely ultimate extrinsic end of the universe because He alone is the Highest Good and absolutely independent. He is Pure Act. He does not acquire the good in any way because He is Goodness Itself. But He communicates the good which is manifested in His creatures objectively. Rational creatures in knowing the excellence of creation praise the Cause of Causes and End of ends. Glory consists objectively in the manifestation of the goodness of God in His creation. Formally, it consists in the knowledge with praise which is given to God by His rational creatures as they contemplate the order and beauty of the universe.

How can we reconcile the judgment: "All mobile beings act for the glory of God" with the facts of physical evil in the universe? Physical evil such as the corruption of a compound, the death of an animal and so forth are not something positive. Physical evil is the absence of a perfection which should be had by a particular nature.[1] The corruption of material things, which for the individual thing must be considered an evil, is for the good of the universe. The lower is subordinated to the higher. God in causing a higher good, namely, the perfection of the universe, causes *per accidens* the corruption of material things which for the individual thing is an evil but which contributes to the order of nature, and the glory of God. What God intends is not the evil as evil but the good of the universe and His glory.

II. THE INTERMEDIATE END OF THE UNIVERSE

Every mobile being seeks its own perfection, and the perfection of the whole universe is obtained through the perfection of the creatures that compose it. Mobile beings attain their ends by acting according to nature's laws. By procuring their ends they produce the perfection of the universe which is governed by its laws.

The intermediary end of the universe is the perfection of man as a rational animal. The lower is subservient to the higher. Man needs and uses the minerals, plants and animals to sustain life and to procure his well-being. It follows that the natural progress of man is in the knowledge and use of the things of

---

[1] *S. Theol.* P. 1, q. 48, a. 3.

nature for the sustenance and welfare of man. In seeking this end, however, man does not realize his natural ultimate destiny unless his life embraces the knowledge and praise of the Author of nature.

The chemist and the physicist in exploring more deeply the structures and functions of the mobile, the engineer in devising and executing new uses of materials, all men of science and technics together with their fellow men, contribute toward true progress not by mere discoveries and conquests in the material world; but, formally, in so far as these reveal to man the power of their Creator and His glory, as the Cause of Causes manifested through the grandeur of nature. In so far as a materialistic commercialism and a totalitarian nationalism tyrannize the sciences this noble destiny is seriously hampered.

Professor Burtt in his critical analysis of *The Metaphysical Foundations of Modern Physical Science* speaks of a new evaluation of man's place in the universe.[1] In view of the discovery of a heliocentric universe it is supposed that man and his planet are no longer the center of consideration but rather occupy a puny place in the universe. But the primary place of man in the universe is by no means disturbed by the fact that our planet is now known not to be the central body around which the other planets revolve.

The Thomist formally views man to be the first creature of importance in the visible universe because man alone is rational and, therefore, has dominion over all other beings of the universe. This evaluation is indifferent to the position of the planet Earth. As St. Thomas says, "Intelligent nature alone in the universe is in request for its own sake; all other creatures on account of it."[2]

If inter-planetary travel should discover other rational animals in the universe besides man on earth, this would prove that the intermediate end of the universe is to be found also in other rational animals beyond our world. In fact it might become evident that such creatures have realized the intermediate finality of the universe more perfectly than man on earth. This would be true if they are superior intellectually and morally to the rational creatures of our planet.

[1] E. Burtt. *The Metaphysical Foundations of Modern Physical Science* (New York: Harcourt, Brace and Co., 1932), pp. 300-301.
[2] *Contra Gentiles,* Bk. 3, ch. 112.

Scholastic philosophers have speculated on this problem long before our contemporary thinkers who are supposing what kind of worlds our space-ships will discover. In his *Summa Theologica* St. Thomas considers the possibility of rational creatures on another heavenly body.[1] Reason cannot negate the possibility of such creatures.

Modern astronomers know that Mars and Venus have atmospheres comparable with that of earth. Photographs of these planets were made with the world's largest telescope on Palomar Mountain, California and recently the first closeup picture of Mars was made by the space-craft Mariner IV. The kind of animal or vegetable life that we know on earth probably could not exist on Venus. There is little or no free oxygen and almost no water on this planet but carbon dioxide is in its atmosphere. Mars probably could not support higher forms of life. It is probable, however, that in the not too distant future, this problem will be answered by interplanetary communication in spaceships. The essential order of Thomistic cosmology would not be affected if another race of rational animals were discovered on another heavenly body.

III. THE RELATIVE PERFECTION OF THE UNIVERSE

The perfection of the universe is relative and not absolute. By a perfect being is meant that to which nothing is absent of those things which are due to it. Absolute perfection is true of God alone. He is the being Who possesses all perfection. The universe is said to be relatively perfect in that nothing is lacking to it in a determined genus. The universe could be more perfect, but it possesses the degree of perfection due to it. Leibniz opposed this view and taught that this is the best possible world. Schopenhauer, on the other hand, said that it would be better if the world did not exist.

The perfection of the universe cannot be absolute, for in producing a finite effect the Divine Exemplar is not exhausted. Omnipotence is not limited to a particular finite world—which limitation would be the case if this is the best possible world. What God wills He obtains infallibly because He is Omnipotent. Now God intends the universe in a degree of perfection determined by Him, and so the universe infallibly represents a

---

[1] *S. Theol.*, P. 3, q. 3, a. 5 and a. 7.

perfection according to a degree which God assigns to it—a degree of goodness, a relative perfection.

It is not uncommon in contemporary times for our adversaries to admit that the evolving universe is relatively perfect but they view this relative perfection solely in the light of the universe itself. Professor Alexander speaks of the universe as a kind of evolving deity.

> God as actually possessing deity does not exist, but as an ideal, is always becoming; but God as the whole universe tending toward deity does exist.[1]

On the contrary, the relative perfection of the universe can never become identified with the divine. Otherwise, one would have to suppose an ever evolving series of contingencies as self-sufficient. As we have seen a contingent series can never satisfy the concept of the divine. It would be a journey without destiny, a becoming without ontological sufficiency. This kind of dynamic pantheism is current in contemporary, materialistic, evolutionary theories.

Belief in this world as the destiny of man produced the Frustrated Man of modern times. We cite here one example of the "sad and sorry picture." Professor Conklin writes:

> If we place in the sharpest possible contrast the old and new conceptions as to the nature of man ... we have a sad and sorry picture. According to the old view he was made in the image of God, according to the new in the image of beasts; once he was said to be a little lower than the angels, now a little higher than the apes....[2]

He who attacks God as the Supreme Efficient Cause and Ultimate End of the Universe attacks man and the very universe itself. He who wages such an attack is a fool, and his weapons are not the weapons of true science but the follies of the fool. It is for this reason that the Scripture does not say that a man has said in his mind there is no God, but "the fool has said in his heart: There is no God."[3]

---

[1] S. Alexander, "Some Explanations," *Mind* (London: October, 1921), p. 428.
[2] *Science* (Lancaster, Penna.: Business Press, Nov. 1928), p. 466.
[3] Ps. 13: 1.

Suggested Reading

St. Thomas Aquinas. *Summa Theologica*, P. 1, q. 44, a. 4; q. 65, a. 2; *Contra Gentiles*, Bk. 3, chs. 17-23.

H. Meyer, *The Philosophy of St. Thomas Aquinas*, translated by F. Eckhoff (St. Louis: Herder Co., 1946), p. 307.

W. D. Ross, *Aristotle* (Cambridge: University Press, 1906), pp. 78-81.

Questions

1. State the thesis on the ultimate end of the universe.
   a. Define the terms.
   b. Who are the opponents?
   c. Prove the thesis.
2. Write an essay on man, the intermediate end of the cosmos and show how this is opposed by many contemporary trends of thought.
3. Is the perfection of the cosmos relative or abosolute? Prove your answer.
4. Compare the view of a universe without meaning to the teleological conception of the universe presented in this chapter.

CONCLUSION

COSMOLOGY TERMINATES in the philosophical knowledge of mobile being in its four causes. It does not end in discovery by analysis but in understanding through synthesis. In the first degree of abstraction we comprehended the most common properties of mobile being and proceeded from these to the essence of mobile being, its intrinsic causes, and then to the knowledge of the extrinsic causes, the origin and destiny of the mobile. The general conclusion of our course, therefore, is the understanding of mobile being as *being in sensible matter and motion composed essentially from prime matter and substantial form by God, the Creator, for His glory.*

The unique contribution of cosmology in the college curriculum is that it offers the student a rationally integrated knowledge of the cosmos in the light of first principles. For the average college student this introduction to a philosophy of nature is all that he can hope to achieve in a lifetime in this field of study. It is consequently the task of a cosmology course to equip the student with an adequate foundation not only in the perennial principles of mobile being but also in the understanding of these by the twentieth century student. Contemporary instance and analogy must be employed to convey the perennial principles in the context of our times. It is hoped that this text has achieved that end.

The philosophy of St. Thomas Aquinas is itself timeless and unchanging in the truth of its universal first principles. New opponents, however, appear from age to age. The materialism of David of Dinant is now replaced by the dialectical materialism of Marx and Lenin. Dynamism once taught by Heraclitus is now evidenced in the systems of the modern energists. In the age of Aquinas, philosophy enjoyed the central place in the faculty of arts. It is now replaced in many centers of learning by technology. Thomistic cosmology in the twentieth century confronts new attacks. We have endeavored to answer these objections in the defense of our theses.

The exposition of the perennial principles of Thomistic cosmology and the integration of these with modern scientific data has rendered cosmology the most complex part of Thomistic philosophy. The student is required to understand the profound principles of nature taught by the Angelic doctor and at the same time to know the intricate data of nuclear physics. Throughout the course these difficulties have been taken into account and attempted to be surmounted by the definition of terms used and the ordering of this complex material in the light of the method and object of this science.

The conclusion of cosmology offers the student no direct and immediate contribution toward education for a job. It does equip him in the direction of education for life. The life of man is formally intellectual in that man is a rational animal. Whereas prime matter, substantial form, God the Creator, and the glory of God are not concepts of "dollar value" to use the language of the pragmatist, they are fundamentals in the language of wisdom. Practical life for man is meaningless without the inspiration and direction that comes from true wisdom. Cosmology gives synthesis to the fragmentary reports of the special sciences of nature and their technological consequences; it is completed by the supreme natural wisdom of metaphysics and elevated by the supernatural wisdom of revealed truth.

We conclude with these masterful verses of the prayer of Solomon:

God of my fathers, and Lord of mercy, Who has made all things with Thy word,

And by Thy wisdom has appointed man, that he should have dominion over the creature that was made by Thee,

That he should order the world according to equity and justice and execute justice with an upright heart:

Give me wisdom, that sitteth by Thy throne, and cast me not off from among Thy children.[1]

---

[1] *Wisdom*, 9:1-4.

GLOSSARY OF SCIENTIFIC TERMS

ACCELERATION. The rate of change of velocity.

ALPHA RAY: ALPHA PARTICLE. A minute positively charged particle emitted by various radioactive bodies. It is an atom of helium which has lost two electrons.

ATOM. The smallest particle of an element that can enter into chemical combination.

ATOMIC MASS UNIT (A.M.U.) A unit adopted for estimating the mass of any atom.

ATOMIC WEIGHT. The weight of the atom in terms of atomic mass units.

BETA RAY: BETA PARTICLE. A very light particle emitted by certain radioactive bodies. It has the same mass and charge as the electron.

CENTIMETER. The hundredth part of a meter. It is very nearly equal to two-fifths of an inch.

CHARGE ELECTRIC. An excess of one kind of electricity over the opposite kind within a body. It is called positive, if positive electricity is in excess. It is called negative, if negative electricity is in excess.

COSMIC RAYS. These are extremely penetrating particles or rays of high energy which come into our atmosphere from the outer spaces of the cosmos.

CYCLOTRON. An apparatus for speeding up charged particles by successive impulses imparted to them by a rapidly alternating electrical field.

DENSITY. The amount of mass per unit of volume.

DISINTEGRATION OF AN ATOM. The decomposition of the nucleus of the atom so that a new kind of atom results.

ELECTROLYSIS. A chemical process which occurs at the surface of contact between a conductor and an electrolyte when a direct current passes from one to the other.

ELECTROLYTE. A liquid in which there are positive and negative carriers of electricity of atomic or molecular dimensions.

ELECTROMAGNETIC. This term is applied to phenomena in which electricity is in motion producing magnetic effects.

ELECTRON. A very small particle about 1/1840 of the mass of the hydrogen atom. It is found in all atoms and has a uniform negative charge.

ENERGY. The capacity for doing work, that is, for producing a force and causing displacement in the direction of the force.

GAMMA RAYS. Electromagnetic rays of very high frequency and short wave length sent out by certain radioactive substances.

KINETIC THEORY. The theory that states that the molecules of all gases are in rapid motion, colliding frequently with one another and with the walls of the containing vessel.

MESOTRON. A particle which shows itself in cosmic rays, having a mass between 150 and 250 times that of the electron.

METER. A fundamental unit of length in the metric system. It is equal to about 39.3 inches.

MOLECULAR THEORY. The theory that all material substances are made up of separate particles called molecules.

MOLECULE. The smallest portion of a chemical compound or of an element which can exist by itself and have the properties of that compound or element.

NEUTRAL. Uncharged, having the two kinds of electricity present in equal amounts and properly distributed.

NEUTRON. A body having a mass nearly equal to that of the hydrogen atom but which has no charge. It comes from the nucleus of various atoms.

NUCLEUS. The part of the atom at its center which contains all the positive charge of the atom and practically all of its mass.

PERIODIC TABLE. One of a number of tables in which the chemical elements are arranged, in the order of their ascending atomic numbers, in horizontal rows of about eight each, one row below the other. The elements of each of the vertical group resulting are like each other in many of their chemical and physical properties.

PHOTON. A single quantum of light radiation.

POSITRON. A positively charged small particle of the same mass as the electron and unit charge.

PROTON. It may mean the nucleus of the hydrogen atom having unit positive charge. It can also mean an elementary particle of the same mass and charge.

QUANTUM THEORY OF ENERGY AND RADIATION. This theory maintains that in all atomic or molecular processes involving emission or absorption of energy, the energy is transferred in separate portions or quanta, the magnitude of which is equal to a constant multiplied by the frequency.

RADIATION. The propagation of energy through space or through matter in the form of electromagnetic waves.

RADIOACTIVITY. A property of certain elements by which they spontaneously emit from the nucleus of the atoms charged particles: alpha or beta rays, or gamma rays.

REST MASS. The mass of a small body at rest or moving with moderate speed as compared with its mass when it is moving with a considerable fraction of the speed of light.

SPECTRUM. A band of light effected by sending light through a prism or other dispersing apparatus and spreading apart the separate radiations of which it is composed. The dimensions of the band depend upon the shape and size of the source of light which is generally a narrow rectangular slit.

TRANSMUTATION. A change of one chemical element into another effected through either natural or artificial radioactivity.

VACUUM. A space from which a very large part or nearly all the original air or other gas has been removed. The vacuum is said to be high when the pressure of the gas is very low.

X-RAYS. Electromagnetic waves of very short wave length and high frequency sent out from the place where rapidly moving electrons are suddenly stopped by a solid such as a heavy metal. They are very penetrating.

Index of Names

Albert, Saint, 45, 150
Alexander, S., 26, 142, 182
Andronicus, 21
Archimedes, 20
Aristotle, 9, 11, 13, 14, 21, 33, 38,
    60, 63, 76, 77, 111, 149, 150,
    151, 164
Augustine, Saint, 33, 150
Avicebron, 126

Bacon, F., 160
Bacon, R., 18, 41, 126
Bergson, H., 79, 88, 165
Berkeley, G., 55
Blavatsky, 92
Blondel, M., 165
Boethius, 84
Bohr, 131
Boscovich, G., 97
Boyle, R., 143
Brahma, 142
Buchner, F., 144
Burtt, E., 180
Butler, S., 112

Cajetan, 134
Cantor, G., 50
Carbonelle, 97
Carnap, R., 35
Chadwick, J., 102
Chamberlain-Moulton, 153
Channing, W., 92
Clarke, J., 117
Conklin, E., 182
Cremonini, C., 24

Darwin, C., 163
Democritus, 94, 143, 160
Descartes, R., 35, 41, 62, 63, 68,
    69, 86, 94, 160
Dewey, J., 76
Dirac, P., 155, 156
Durandus, 44

Eddington, A., 62, 83, 96
Eddy, M., 91
Einstein, A., 50, 57-59, 82-84, 96,
    132, 167, 172
Emerson, R., 92
Engels, F., 91, 97

Ferrara, 134
Fichte, J., 91, 142
Fleming, S., 81
Foley, L., 103
Frank, P., 169
Fuller, M., 92

Galileo, G., 23, 86
Gassendi, P., 79, 94
Gilson, E., 94
Gredt, J., 48
Grosseteste, R., 126

Haeckel, E., 91
Haldane, 17
Harnack, A., 174
Hartmann, E., 97
Hegel, G., 76, 142
Heisenberg, W., 165, 166-167
Heraclitus, 76, 97
Hobbes, T., 18
Holbach, d', 144
Hoyle, F., 10, 152-155
Hume, D., 69, 88
Hutchins, R., 72, 73
Huxley, T., 144

James, W., 88
Jeans, 62
Joffe, A., 17
John of Peckham, 126
John of St. Thomas, 134

Kant, I., 55, 79, 88, 152, 160
Kepler, 86
Kronecker, 50

Laplace, 152
Lemaitre, A., 153
Leibnitz, G., 10, 47, 97, 99
Leucippus, 94, 143
Lobatchowsky, 57
Lomanitz, G., 98
Lotze, R., 97

Mach, E., 17, 72, 97
Maeterlinck, M., 143
Maimonides, 150
Maritain, J., 89
Marx, K., 26, 97, 165

Index of Subjects